PROJECT MANAGEMENT

The people challenge

Roland and Frances Bee

INSTITUTE OF PERSONNEL AND DEVELOPMENT

This book is dedicated to our parents/parents-in-law:
Molly Elaine Bevan, 1914–1996
John Cledwyn Bevan, 1912–1991

First published in 1997

Reprinted 1998

Design by Paperweight
Typeset by Action Publishing Technology, Gloucester
Printed in Great Britain by
the Cromwell Press, Trowbridge, Wiltshire

British Library Cataloguing in Publication Data
A catalogue record for this book is available from the British Library

ISBN 0-85292-661-8

**INSTITUTE OF PERSONNEL
AND DEVELOPMENT**

IPD House, Camp Road, London SW19 4UX
Tel: 0181 971 9000   Fax: 0181 263 3333
Registered office as above. Registered Charity No. 1038333
A company limited by guarantee. Registered in England No. 2931892

CONTENTS

LIST OF FIGURES AND TABLES

Figures

Tables

ACKNOWLEDGEMENTS

We would like to thank all the following for their help and support in contributing case-study material for our book, which provided invaluable insights into the people challenges of project management in their organisations:

Keith Bater, Manager Business Processes, Rank Xerox
Joanna May, Personnel Director, ICL Enterprises, ICL
Christine Porter, Principal Lecturer, Faculty of BMSS, University of Westminster
Tony Reid, Chairman of the Project Organisation and Team Working Group of the Association of Project Management
Gordon Roberts, Head of Production Services, Eastern Group plc
Mark Robinson, Group Strategy Adviser, Eastern Group plc
Mike Vessey, Senior Consultant, London Transport Strategic HR Unit
David Whitfield, Director of Project Management, ICL

1

WHAT ARE PROJECT TEAMS (AND WHY ARE WE INTERESTED IN THEM)?

Introduction

More and more organisations are adopting project working approaches for an increasingly diverse range of activities. A number of factors is influencing this trend:

☐ Organisations are now operating in increasingly turbulent environments, where the pace of change on all fronts – technology, customer expectations, competition – marches relentlessly on and where flexibility and the ability to respond to these changes can make the difference between life and death for an organisation. The traditional rigid organisational structures, with their strong demarcations between specialisms and where communication channels are designed to work vertically up and down the hierarchies, make it difficult for organisations to respond quickly and effectively to change. Project working sets out to establish horizontal links between different specialisms.

☐ The increasing complexity of tasks, combined with shorter time-scales, has generated the need for cross-functional and multidisciplinary teams that can be set up quickly to carry out a specific task and then be disbanded when the task is completed.

☐ The increasing pressure on resources has resulted in organisations needing to use their resources most effectively, with clear links between outputs and inputs. The project approach, with its clear goals and systems for monitoring resources, meets this need.

☐ An increasingly skilled workforce, with rising expectations and needs for work that provides high levels of job satisfaction, is looking for opportunities to work in creative and flexible environments. Project working can often provide this type of stimulating environment.

This book looks at how this relatively new and developing way of working for many organisations affects the people that work in and with project teams. It looks at the people challenges posed by project working and how these challenges can be managed to get the best results from and for the individual, team, and organisation.

While this book is intended both for all those who are involved with leading and working in or with project teams, it is also aimed at the human resource (HR) professional who can play a crucial role in ensuring that the people implications of project working are addressed. It is based on our experience as leaders and members of project teams ourselves, working with organisations using this style of operation, and on case-studies of five organisations undertaken specifically for this book. These are described at the end of this chapter.

What you will gain from reading *Project management: the people challenge* are *strategies* to help you:

☐ put together effective project teams
☐ get project teams up and running quickly by establishing sound team processes
☐ ensure that project teams deliver the results through motivating and managing the performance of team members
☐ wind down the teams at the end of the project in such a way that it is seen by all those involved as a positive move onwards and forwards.

Let's start at the beginning and clarify what we mean by a *project*.

What is a project?

The characteristics of projects, which differentiate them from other activities or undertakings in an organisation, usually centre around four themes. Projects:

☐ are clearly goal-oriented – usually with very specific objectives

☐ involve co-ordinating a number of interrelated activities – often across functional boundaries

☐ are of finite duration – they will start and finish

☐ are all in some way unique.

Most of us are familiar with the traditional concept of projects – such as construction projects, ranging from small ones, eg building a conservatory, to massive undertakings like the building of the Channel Tunnel. We have seen the advance of projects into areas such as software development, development of new products, and the implementation of new systems and organisations. We are increasingly seeing major cultural and organisational change being introduced through project structures and management.

For many organisations project structures are set up to deal with specific issues or needs and are bolted onto the main organisational structures. Good examples of these are found in our case-studies of Eastern Group, which set up projects to handle a specific investment opportunity and a major change initiative, and in Rank Xerox, which used the project approach to undertake a far-reaching internal reorganisation study.

Other organisations use projects as a way of managing the great majority of their activities, whereby project working becomes a way of life. The construction industry provides the obvious example here. However, the approach is extending far beyond this traditional sector of project management; for example, our case-study of International Computer Ltd's (ICL) Enterprises business, where solutions work for clients, is all organised on a project basis and, perhaps more unusually, the Strategic HR Unit of London Transport (LT) took a policy decision to apply project working principles to all their work.

Then there are organisations where forms of project working are in place, but where this is less overt – for example, our case-study on the University of Westminster's Business, Management and Social Sciences (BMSS) Faculty. There, *ad hoc* teams are set up to deal with specific issues such as the development or review of a new programme, such as an MBA. However, a longer-term structure is also in operation where, in addition to the main organisational teams (based on Schools and Subject Area Teams which are structured by specialisms such as Finance or HR), there are cross-functional teams drawn from the various Subject Area Teams which manage the individual programmes or courses offered by the University.

It is worth pausing a moment at this point to bring in another term or set of terms that is often used in conjunction with project working: *matrix* organisations and *matrix* teams. The classic organisational design is based on the principle of departmentalisation, which groups the activities of an organisation by, for example:

☐ function, eg a manufacturing organisation structured by production, sales, finance, etc
☐ product or service, eg a supermarket organisation structured according to fruit and vegetables, meat, fish, dry goods, etc
☐ customer, eg consultancies structured by private- and public-sector clients
☐ location, eg the NHS, which is structured into Regional Health Authorities.

Such classic structures are characterised by clear hierarchies and concepts such as unity of command, ie people have only one boss. The matrix structure, by contrast, allows for the organisation to be structured in more than one way and explicitly breaks the concept of unity of command, allowing for the possibility of multiple command systems – in other words an individual having more than one boss. Organisations will often have a traditional departmentalised structure but, in addition, people will work in other structures based on projects or programmes. (See Davis and Lawrence (1977) for a full description of matrix organisations.)

In our case-study of the BMSS Faculty of the University of Westminster, the organisational structure of Schools and

Subject Area Teams described earlier is overlaid by a programme structure based on the different educational programmes offered by the Faculty. The programme teams will be made up of people working from the different Schools and Subject Area Teams. Each member of staff could belong to several programme teams and therefore report to several *programme managers* as well as to their School manager. This is a semi-permanent structure, in that individuals could work on the same programmes indefinitely, although in practice they change programmes from time to time.

In the case of the change project in Eastern Group, the team members were mainly full time on that project for a specified period. In the case of the LT Strategic HR Unit, an individual could be working on one or several projects at the same time for specified periods. In both these cases the structures are temporary, set up solely to deal with that particular project. However, the key feature of all matrix-type structures is that the individuals who work in them have more than one manager: their departmental manager and their project manager. For clarity, in the rest of the book we shall use the terms:

- □ *home manager* to refer to the departmental manager, who might be the functional manager, eg the finance manager, or the product/service manager, eg furniture manager, because in most project/matrix set-ups the individual is based in a 'home' department
- □ *project leader* to describe the person charged with the responsibility of achieving the project objectives (called the 'project manager' in some organisations)
- □ *project manager/administrator* to describe the person responsible for managing the project planning, monitoring, and control processes (this role is often taken by the project leader, particularly for small projects)
- □ *stable team* to describe a traditional departmental or functional team
- □ *project team* to describe a team of people brought together to work on a specific project.

What is different about project teams?

We set off talking about projects and project structures; the next question relates to what the key differences are between project teams and other teams. Hardingham and Royal (1994) in their excellent account of teamwork quote several definitions from the *Oxford English Dictionary* of a team but plump for 'a number of persons associated in *some joint action*'. Frame (1995) uses a similar but subtly different definition to describe a project team as 'a collection of individuals who work together *to attain a goal*'. Whereas traditional functional or departmental teams will be working together on some joint action, the project team will generally be focused on a specific goal. Geddes, Hastings and Briner (1990) describe project teamworking as 'organisational teamworking' and distinguish it from the more traditional teamworking models by means of the following characteristics:

□ 'brought together for a specific project', ie to achieve a specific goal

□ 'team members seldom work full time on the project', with the result that they may have conflicting priorities and loyalties

□ 'non-hierarchical team members' – they may not be under the control of the project leader and indeed could be of a higher status in organisational terms

□ 'cross-functional' – they frequently consist of members drawn from across different parts of the organisation

□ there are 'both "visible" and "invisible" team members'. The project's achievement will often depend not just on the work of the formal project team members, ie the visible members, but also on a whole raft of other people – the sponsor or client of the project (more of these roles later), suppliers and subcontractors, and functional colleagues of the visible members. These often form quite a large invisible team which is vital to the success of the project. All of these are *stakeholders* in various forms in the project. The concept of stakeholders is important in project working because it emphasises the number and diversity of people who both 'have a stake in the success of the undertaking'

(Whitfield, 1995) and who will also influence the outcome. We would add two other key characteristics:

☐ The team often has to be up and running very quickly and effectively to meet tight project deadlines.
☐ Individual job descriptions usually do not exist for project team members in the way they do in stable teams. This can add ambiguity, uncertainty, and role conflict for team members.

All these characteristics have implications for the effective management of project teams. There are many books (eg, Lockyer, 1984) that talk about the mechanics of managing the projects in terms of cost, time, and specification. They focus primarily on the planning and control tools, such as network analysis and Gantt charts. This book concentrates on the challenges of managing the key resource of people – the visible and invisible team – on whose efforts the success of the project depends. Many organisations have adopted project/matrix approaches in response to particular needs but without necessarily thinking through the implications for:

☐ the project team members – ie, what the issues and pressures for them that result from project team/matrix working are
☐ the project leader – ie, what the management and leadership issues that arise from this style of working are
☐ the rest of the organisation – ie, how the rest of the organisation reacts and responds to the use of project teams
☐ the HR professional and the systems that support the human side of any enterprise – ie, what the role of the HR professional is, how performance management reviews are conducted when there is more than one boss, and who identifies training and development needs.

To understand the nature of project working three important and related concepts should be introduced at this stage:

☐ the project life cycle
☐ the project team life cycle
☐ the team development cycle.

The three cycles of project teamworking

Every *project* has a life cycle, which is commonly described as having four phases:

1   project conception/definition
2   planning and resourcing
3   implementation
4   termination/rundown.

The *project team* has a similar and interrelated life cycle, which forms the structure of this book:

☐   putting the project team together (Chapter 2) – selecting the project leader and recruiting the team

☐   getting the project team working (Chapter 3) – which addresses the issues of aligning objectives, establishing team processes, and building effective relationships within the context of the project

☐   delivering results through the project team (Chapter 4) – which examines the issues of how performance is managed, how the team is motivated and rewarded, and how short-term (project) and long-term (personal) training and development needs are identified

☐   moving onwards (Chapter 5) – planning for the completion of the project, celebrating success, evaluating performance and learning from it, dismantling the team, and reallocating team members.

The relationship between these two cycles is set out below. The traditional focus has been on the *project* life cycle; we shall argue that equal attention should be given to the *project team* life cycle.

Project conception/definition

Projects arise in a whole variety of ways. They can be stimulated from the external environment, eg in the Eastern Group case-study the opportunity arose to bid for a share in an overseas company, and in ICL projects are set up to meet specific customer needs. Alternatively, they can be stimulated by the internal environment, as in the Eastern Group business process re-engineering (BPR) project and the Rank Xerox reorganisation project. This first phase is crucial, when the project takes on a clear identity and focus. Three key interrelated questions need to be answered at this point:

☐ What are the objectives of the project?
☐ What are the outputs?
☐ What are the success criteria against which the project will be assessed?

Not only does this first phase provide the vital foundations on which all the other stages will depend, but finding the answers to the above questions can also have a major impact on the successful working of the project team. Bater of Rank Xerox used the following Biblical quotation to emphasise the importance of having a clear vision for the project and communicating it to all concerned.

> If the trumpet give forth an uncertain sound, who shall prepare to the battle?
>
> St Paul, 1 Corinthians 14: 8

We shall talk about the significance of this statement in Chapter 3, when we discuss the need to align the organisation, project, team, and individuals' objectives, and in Chapter 4 on the motivational issues arising out of project working.

The second set of questions to be answered at this stage relates to identifying the key stakeholders in the project: who the sponsors or customers for the project are. For example, the Eastern Group investment project was sponsored by an executive director, but the customer was the whole board. In ICL the project would have a sponsor within the appropriate business unit of ICL, whereas the customer would be the external client representative. These are the key players in clarifying and agreeing the scope of the project.

It is at the end of this stage that the project leader will usually be appointed (although he or she may also have been involved in the project definition stage). The core project team will often be set up at this point as well. This is the stage in the project team cycle covered in Chapter 2.

Planning and resourcing

Having decided *what* is to be done, the next phase concerns the *how* it is done. The first step is usually the preparation of a project plan setting out:

☐ the detailed tasks or activities that need to be completed for the successful completion of the whole project

☐ the time-scales for undertaking these activities, including key milestones in the project

☐ the resources – cost, people, equipment, etc – required to complete each activity

☐ who is responsible for each activity.

However, equally important, and what we suggest should actually be the first steps, are:

☐ establishing how the team will work – in other words, setting up the team processes

☐ ensuring that the team members have the key personal skills to work effectively together.

This is the stage in the project team life cycle covered in Chapter 3.

Implementation

This is the culmination of the first two phases, what the team has been preparing and working for: actually carrying out the work of the project. In traditional project management theory, the emphasis is now on controlling the project: monitoring progress against the plan in terms of the three key parameters of specification, time, and cost, and taking appropriate action to keep the project on plan or amending the plan and reporting back.

In the project team life cycle, this is the 'delivering results' stage, and the issues central to Chapter 4 are the HR issues of managing individuals' and the team's performance, including the handling of performance problems, training and development, and motivation and reward.

Termination/rundown

This is the phase when the project draws to a close. The key activities concern ensuring that the objectives have been achieved, the outputs delivered, and the success criteria met.

One of the problems of this stage in the project life cycle can be that most of the interesting and challenging work has been completed and the remaining, often *housekeeping*, tasks can be time-consuming and tedious. However, in some projects this will be a crucial phase involving the handover of the project to the client, as for example in the development of new software systems. This is the phase where proper planning of the rundown of the team and the smooth reallocation of team members can play such an important part in maintaining motivation. It is also the phase of team development when the learning opportunities from working on the project can be realised. These are the central features of the final stage of the project team life cycle covered in the last chapter of this book.

Before we leave the issue of the project team life cycle it is important to draw in the third cycle – often referred to as the growth or developmental cycle. This theory in its original form proposed that every team, like an individual, will go through a series of stages before it reaches maturity (for further discussion, see Handy (1977) and Woodcock (1979)). These are the:

☐ *forming* stage – when the team is not yet a team but a collection of individuals. At this stage the members will discuss relatively superficial, non-contentious issues such as the title and life span of the team. The individual members are trying to create an initial impression. This stage is often characterised by what Hardingham and Royal (1994) refer to as 'an artificially polite atmosphere'.

☐ *storming* stage – as the title suggests, a time of conflict and turbulence in the team, when previous agreements, often reached on a superficial basis during the first stage, are challenged. The resulting consensus is usually more realistic and long-lasting. It is a time when individual members begin to show their personal agendas and push back the boundaries of acceptable behaviour. It is regarded as a crucial stage for building and testing team cohesion. Often teams try to avoid it as it is an uncomfortable stage, but research shows that teams that try to avoid it and go directly to the next stage usually have their storming stage later!

- □ *norming* stage – when the team begins to establish norms and practices, often referred to as the 'team processes'. These set a solid foundation for the crucial next stage.
- □ *performing* stage – reached only when the previous three stages have been successfully completed and the team has reached *maturity*. Some level of performance will be achieved during the earlier stages, but this is when the team will be operating at optimum effectiveness. Members will have learned to challenge the right issues in the appropriate way, handle conflict in a constructive manner, support and help each other, and manage change.

An additional stage is now acknowledged as teams become more transient entities:

- □ *mourning* stage – when teams learn to handle their own demise at the end of the project. This stage is often overlooked – after all, the project has been completed, so what does it matter what happens to the team? This is a short-sighted view on two counts. First, with many projects there is no clean finish and there will be many tidying-up and follow-up activities to be completed. Secondly, working in a successfully performing team usually involves building sound and productive personal relationships between members, and requires considerable and sustained energy and commitment. It is important that members move on to their next project in a positive frame of mind and that those useful relationships, often developed at some cost, are maintained as part of the individuals' network of information and support.

In practice, most teams do not pass through these stages in an orderly fashion; they may loop back through some of the stages many times. The stages of forming, storming, and norming will play a crucial part in the 'getting the team working' phase; the performing stage is clearly aligned with the 'delivering results' phase; and the mourning stage is aligned likewise with the 'moving onward' phase. The characteristics of project teams (as set out previously) put particular and peculiar stresses on the normal team development stages – for example, such stresses as the short time-scales for the team to reach the performing stage, the pressures of members' being part of more than one team, and the sometimes more complex power and authority relationships.

As a summary, the links between these three cycles are set out in Table 1.

Table 1

LINKS BETWEEN PROJECT, PROJECT TEAM, AND TEAM DEVELOPMENT CYCLES

Project life cycle	Project team cycle	Team development cycle
Project conception/definition	Putting the project team together (Chapter 2)	
Planning and resourcing	Getting the project team working (Chapter 3)	Forming, storming, norming
Implementation	Delivering results in the project matrix (Chapter 4)	Performing
Termination/rundown	Moving onwards (Chapter 5)	Mourning

About the case-studies

We chose organisations that we knew were using project working at that time as a key part of their strategy for business success. They are all large organisations – because it is in the large organisations that the pressures of this way of working are highlighted and the issues brought into sharpest relief. Many small organisations use forms of project working, but one of the strengths and advantages of small organisations is that the resulting issues can be dealt with more informally. However, this book, based on our experience as practitioners and the results of this research, will have relevance to all sizes of organisations as they seek to improve the efficiency and effectiveness of their activities through project teamworking.

Eastern Group

The Eastern Group is one of the main energy providers in the UK. Historically, its principal business has been the distribution and supply of electricity to three million customers in Eastern England – through Eastern Electricity. The Group also includes Eastern Generation, which owns, operates, and develops power stations, and Eastern Natural Gas, the second largest independent supplier of gas in the UK. The Eastern Group has undergone, and is still going through, a major period of change – starting with the deregulation of the energy industry, then its acquisition by Hanson in September 1995, and now the demerger from Hanson, which has seen Eastern Group merged with Peabody, a major coal producer, and launched as a separate company, the Energy Group.

Project working is used to tackle specific issues. We looked at two examples:

□ The first project examined the potential to acquire a stake in a substantial overseas energy company and prepare the associated tender bid. This was a relatively short project spanning a few weeks and involving a project team that ranged between 25 and 30 members. The team was made up of a mixture of internal staff – some working full time on the project, others only part time – and outside consultants.

□ The second was the *Apple* project, which spearheaded the business process re-engineering (BPR) of Eastern's operations. This was an 18-month project with a project team of about 20 people. The team was a mix of internal Eastern Group staff and consultants, all working full time on the project but not necessarily for the whole of the project.

Mark Robinson, group strategy adviser, the project leader for the first project, and Gordon Roberts, head of production services, the project leader for the Apple project, were our contacts in Eastern Group.

London Transport Strategic HR Unit

London Transport (LT) encompasses London Underground Ltd and is also responsible for the procurement of bus services in London. It employs over 18,000 people. In an advertisement

(*People Management*, 12 September 1996) the role of the Unit was described as follows:

> Our goals for the year 2000 are ambitious and people are the critical element of our change programme. Our Strategic HR Unit designs and implements these programmes, operating on a project management basis delivering a diverse range of activities across the business.

The Unit is about 70 strong and is organised into three teams:

- the Strategy Team, which designs policies, programmes, and projects
- the Implementation Team, which implements these policies, programmes, and projects
- the Programme Management Team, which monitors the programmes once they have been implemented.

All the work is organised on a project basis. A project is generated when a customer or board director requests some work be done. Projects can range from small research projects run internally within the HR Unit, for example evaluating a graduate training programme, to major projects such as the one that planned and organised the implementation of the new statutory regulations in the area of alcohol and drugs, which involved staff across the organisation and lasted for over a year.

We talked with several members of the Unit, but Mike Vessey, senior consultant, was our main point of contact.

International Computers Ltd

International Computers Ltd (ICL), in which Fujitsu is now a major stakeholder, employs over 20,000 staff world-wide. ICL has seen a substantial change of direction in recent years in the process of moving, (as David Whitfield, director of project management, put it) 'from shipping boxes [ie computer products] to producing business solutions for its customers, where projects are seen as the delivery vehicle for these solutions'. Projects can range enormously in size and complexity; they may involve fewer than 10 or more than 600 staff, and last from a few months to a few years. Like the LT Strategic HR Unit, working in project teams is the main approach to delivering results. ICL believes that in today's competitive environment its 'track record in effective project management is a key differentiator' (Whitfield, 1995).

ICL has tackled project management in a systematic way. There is a Project Management Board (PMB) which, among other activities, exists

> to establish the policy, and to agree and actively promote effective standards, processes, gradings and careers in Project Management across the ICL Group.
>
> (ICL, 1995)

The PMB has produced a booklet setting out a framework of project management activities to ensure a consistent approach throughout ICL. Project management is viewed as a key career stream for staff at ICL, with a clear grading structure and associated competencies, and well-defined training and development paths.

David Whitfield, director of project management for the ICL Group, and Joanna May, personnel director of ICL Enterprises, were our contacts.

Faculty of Business, Management and Social Studies, University of Westminster

The Faculty of Business, Management and Social Studies (BMSS) primarily runs a range of undergraduate and postgraduate programmes in the general business and management areas. The 170 or so academic staff are organised into four Schools and 13 Subject Area Teams, such as Finance and HR. Overlying this organisational structure are teams that manage the individual programmes, for example the MBA (Master of Business Administration) and DMS (Diploma in Management Studies) programmes. These teams mainly consist of the staff that teach on that particular programme and therefore can be drawn from across all the Subject Area Teams. The teams are semi-permanent and run over the life of the programme, although the staff involved may change. There are also teams set up to tackle specific *ad hoc* projects, such as the development of a new programme or the redesign of a programme. A particular feature of all the teams is that they may involve quite a high proportion of part-time staff, called 'visiting lecturers', who are employed on an hourly basis.

Christine Porter, principal lecturer in the Management School, was our contact at the University of Westminster.

Rank Xerox

Project teams are used in Rank Xerox for a wide range of activities. Some operate on a regular basis, eg for launching a new product or for systems development projects. Others, usually referred to as Quality Improvement Teams, are set up for a specific purpose to solve a particular business problem; for example, one project team was set up to tackle a major business issue – to increase Rank Xerox's Return on Assets from 7 per cent to 18 per cent by 1996. This involved a massive internal benchmarking exercise that spanned Rank Xerox's operations across Europe and the USA. It is the work of this project team that forms the focus of this case-study. The team was drawn from across the international units and across the functions, eg customer service and information management, and operated over an eight-month period.

Keith Bater, manager business processes, was our contact at Rank Xerox.

About our approach

Our approach is based on:

- [ ] our experience of working on and leading project teams on projects as diverse as a major marketing project, a warehouse extension, setting up structures for a new organisation, and introducing new technology and systems
- [ ] working as consultants with a wide range of organisations operating in manufacturing, transportation, retail, and the public sector
- [ ] the research carried out specifically for this book during 1996 – the five case-studies described above
- [ ] looking at the literature on project teamworking and the various theories relevant to teamworking
- [ ] informal research carried out by talking to a number of people involved in project working – a special mention should be made here of Tony Reid, chairman of the Project Organisation and Team Working Group for the Association

of Project Management (APM) and an experienced independent consultant in the project management field.

It will not surprise many people working in the field to find out that there were sometimes considerable gaps between what the *theorists* said ought to happen and what the *practitioners* recounted as actually happening! The very situations that gave rise to the need for project working – the turbulent environment, the pressure on resources, the need for things to happen quickly – also mean that there is sometimes simply not the time or resources to do things in an ideal way. That is not to say it is not possible or desirable to aim for the best-practice approach, but that often a more pragmatic way forward needs to be taken. Success is often based on managing the gap between the ideal and the pragmatic. However, there is also concern that projects are not as successful as they might be:

> ... a remarkable number of projects ... are not achieving what was expected of them ... twice as many IT projects are considered to be 'less successful' than are considered to be successful.
>
> (Wateridge, 1995)

> The building of the British Library 'could be used as a model of how not to manage a major construction project' according to a report by an all-party group of MPs.
>
> (Woolmer, 1996)

We believe that it is addressing and meeting the people challenge of project working that can make the vital difference. We have set out a number of strategies which we believe meet this people challenge. Some of these strategies are in themselves challenging and offer the opportunity in particular for the HR professional to get more involved. However, for the strategies to work they require everyone involved – the project leader, anyone who works in or with project teams, and in fact all the stakeholders – to decide that they *are* important and to back them.

We are now ready to move on to the first stage of the project team life cycle: putting the team together.

2

PUTTING THE PROJECT
TEAM TOGETHER

Introduction

In Chapter 1 we discussed the background to the use of project teams and set out the concept of phases in the life of a project team. In this chapter we look at the issues involved in the first phase of the project team – putting the project team together and, in particular, the selection of the project leader. We also look at the ongoing issue of managing team changes during the course of the project. We combine our own experience of working with project teams with that of our practitioners, to distil what we see to be the key lessons for managing the people challenges of working in this distinctive area of project teams rather than stable teams. We also examine briefly the work of some writers who have been influential in recent years in the formation of successful teams and comment against this backdrop on the practical issues affecting the setting up of project teams.

We see the key people challenges of this phase as:

☐ forming effective project teams – in combining the pragmatic approach of who is available possessing the right skills and experience with getting a balance of informal team roles

☐ identifying and clarifying the role of the project leader – drawing out the major distinctions in role between leaders of project teams and leaders of stable teams

☐ selecting the right project leader – highlighting the key characteristics of a project leader

☐ Handling changes in project team membership during the life of the project.

Forming effective project teams

In the recruitment of effective teams we, in common with most HR professionals, believe that a systematic approach to selection will give the best chance of making the right selection decisions through, for example:

☐ having a clear, well-researched personnel specification
☐ wide advertising aimed at the appropriate population (internal or external, or both)
☐ good selection techniques, eg skilled interviewing, possible use of assessment centres, psychometric tests, etc.

However, our experience and the evidence presented by those who contributed to our research suggest that this systematic approach is rarely followed in the recruitment of people to *project* teams. With certain exceptions, a pragmatic approach to the selection of project team members seems to prevail: the choice is often constrained by whoever is available with the requisite professional skills and experience. At first sight this might suggest that recruitment and selection is not a major issue but, as we hope to demonstrate, there is plenty of evidence to suggest otherwise. We believe a key issue centres around the concept of what are referred to as *team roles*.

Balancing team roles

Perhaps the seminal piece of research in this area was the work of Meredith Belbin. Belbin and his team (Belbin, 1981) found that consistently successful teams, in addition to covering the professional specialisms or functions required, were made up of a mixture of different personality types. They were able to classify the different types into eight discrete categories which they described as *team roles*: Chairman, Company Worker, Completer-Finisher, Monitor-Evaluator, Plant, Resource Investigator, Shaper, and Team Worker. Belbin later identified a ninth category – the Specialist – and renamed some of the roles. (See Table 2 for details of Belbin's team roles.) Belbin argued that for teams to succeed they needed to have all these team roles covered. It was possible for a person to show a strength in more than one team role; indeed, some people show strengths in three or more – we call these the *generalists*. Such people are very useful in project teams because of their ability to cover gaps that would otherwise occur in the balance of the team.

Belbin's model is useful not just in the selection of teams but also, because most people will have at least some strength in a role other than their primary one, in managing the gaps in team roles of established teams. For example, where there is a lack of the intellectual ideas-person (the Plant), then others with the most strength in that role might determinedly set out to cover that gap.

Our own work with teams from a whole range of organisations also supports the view that a balance of team roles is important. We have found that, based on an analysis of what is going wrong in the team, it is usually possible to predict where the gaps in team roles are. For example, teams that find it difficult to meet deadlines often lack a Completer-Finisher. Teams who find it hard to generate innovative solutions usually lack strength in the Plant role. This was demonstrated very vividly in work we did with managers going through an MBA programme. They were placed randomly into teams and set the task over a weekend of solving an interesting practical exercise, which required creative thinking to find a solution. We did the exercise with nearly 200 managers, and two of the most striking results were how few strong Plants there were among the managers and how teams with little or no strength in this team role struggled to get anywhere with the task.

It is not just a question of identifying the people best qualified professionally in their specialist area and recruiting them into a team framework; the team must be balanced in terms of the mixture of personalities of team members – or the *informal roles* that team members play – in order for the team to be consistently successful in reaching its objectives.

Returning for a moment to the work of Belbin and his colleagues, they included in their research a series of interesting experiments where all the 'best' people were teamed up together. This is particularly relevant in the context of project

Table 2

BELBIN TEAM ROLES

Team type	Team role*	Typical features	Positive qualities	Allowable weaknesses
Company Worker Implementer*	A good organiser turns ideas into practical actions	Conservative, dutiful, predictable	Organising ability, practical common sense, hard worker, self-discipline	Lack of flexibility, unresponsiveness to unproven ideas
Chairman Co-ordinator*	Clarifies goals, co-ordinates, promotes decision-making	Calm, self-confident, controlled	Capacity for welcoming all potential contributors and treating them on their merits without prejudice	No more than ordinary in terms of intellect or creative ability
Shaper	Forces things along, shapes team's efforts, seeing relationships between issues	Highly strung, outgoing, dynamic	Drive and readiness to challenge inertia, ineffectiveness, complacency, or self-deception	Proneness to provocation, irritation, and impatience
Plant	The ideas person, provider of innovative solutions	Individualistic, serious-minded, unorthodox	Genius, imagination, intellect, knowledge	Up in the clouds, inclined to disregard practical details or protocol
Resource Investigator	Explorer of opportunities, developer of outside contacts	Extroverted, enthusiastic, curious, communicative	Capacity for contacting people and exploring anything new, ability to respond to challenge	Liable to lose interest once the initial fascination has passed
Monitor-Evaluator	Analyses and evaluates the options, is accurate judge of things	Sober, unemotional, prudent	Judgement, discretion, hard-headedness	Lacks inspiration or the ability to motivate others
Team Worker	The internal diplomat, listens to all sides, builds, averts friction, calms the waters	Socially oriented, rather mild, sensitive	Ability to respond to people and situations, and to promote team spirit	Indecisiveness at moments of crisis

Completer-Finisher Completer*	Looks after the detail, searches out errors and omissions, delivers on time	Painstaking, orderly, conscientious, anxious	Capacity for follow-through, perfectionism	A tendency to worry about small things, a reluctance to let go
Specialist*	Provides specialist knowledge and skills	Single-minded, self-starting, dedicated	Pre-eminent in his or her field	Contributes only on a narrow front, dwells on technicalities, overlooks the big picture

Based on Belbin (1981) and Belbin (1993)*

teams because, as we shall see later, the recruitment of team members is often on the basis of putting together the *best* group of people with the relevant expertise. In these experiments Belbin set up competing teams where one team was comprised of members who were chosen for their high scores on tests of mental ability. These 'Apollo' teams, as they were called 'out of respect for the American lunar triumph at the time' (Belbin, 1981), then took part in an exercise where people of higher intelligence might have been expected to do better than their less intelligent colleagues. To the surprise of Belbin and his colleagues, and perhaps of most of us, the Apollo teams regularly performed least well. What seemed to the observers of the exercise to be the problem was that each member of an Apollo team was able to spot the flaws in the arguments of others but there was 'no coherence in the decisions the team reached – or was forced to reach – and several pressing and necessary jobs were totally neglected' (Belbin, 1981). The Apollo teams appeared to be difficult to manage, prone to destructive debate, and had difficulties in decision-making. It was not the case that Apollo teams were never successful, but that the factors which appeared to influence their success was the balance of team roles within the team and the style or personality of the person playing the leader role (see later).

So, what are the implications for recruiting a potentially successful team? There appears to be a strong consensus that no matter how skilled and experienced team members are, if there is not a balance of the informal team roles then the team is likely to find it harder to achieve its objectives. Without this balance in the informal roles it is difficult for the team to use their individual knowledge and expertise to the full. However, our research showed that, with the exception of Roberts' BPR project team in Eastern Group, there appears to be little or no attempt to apply this principle of balancing team roles when putting the project teams together – mainly for the pragmatic reasons set out earlier.

How project teams are selected in practice

So what does happen? In Eastern Group, Robinson and Roberts both agreed that 'functional mix' – by which they meant the mixture of professional specialisms of team members – is normally the main driver in putting the project teams together.

There are two approaches to the recruitment of people into their project teams:

- *informal* – members 'gravitate into the project' through interest in the subject or their relationship with the project leader (cf. the University of Westminster model; see later)
- *formal* – they are nominated by their functional manager as available and having the requisite professional competencies (cf. the Rank Xerox/LT models; see later.)

It was suggested that about 60 per cent of recruitment to project teams in Eastern Group is done on the informal basis. Robinson commented that he sees familiar faces in many of his projects – those of people who have a reputation of being able to produce the goods even though they may be busy elsewhere. It is interesting to speculate whether these people have the generalist team profiles discussed earlier or the particular, personal qualities that make them good project team players (see later). Also, there is often a strong bonding between people who have previously worked together successfully on a project, which encourages them to re-form on other projects.

The Eastern Group projects were also different from our other examples in that not only do they have the complexity of recruitment from internal sources but they also regularly recruit specialist outside advisers to their project teams. These external resources can be an unknown quantity and, therefore, present an additional complication to balancing the team.

On the Group's BPR project, some people were appointed on a full-time basis and others on a part-time basis, moving in and out of the core team as required. On this project, there were about 10 people from Eastern Group and 10 outside advisers from a supporting specialist consultancy. A decision was made at board level to recruit the best people to the team (an Apollo team?). This project was the exception to our experience of pragmatic selection. These best people were identified by Roberts, the project leader, and his director colleagues, targeted for interview and psychometric testing, and selected against a written specification. Team members were essentially hand-picked by the project leader working in conjunction with their functional directors. What Roberts wanted, he explained, was people who matched the specification in terms of qualifications and experience *and* who could be expected to gel together on the basis of their Belbin profiles. They were also to be people who were 'difficult to release' because of their value to their existing functions (Roberts' way of ensuring he got the best!). The successful candidates came from all levels across the business and were all 'fit for the purpose', ie they had appropriate qualifications and experience.

On Eastern's acquisitions project, which was relatively short, team membership was largely full time. Robinson commented that the Belbin approach was not widely used in the setting up of project groups in Eastern. He had not attempted to balance team roles in his projects but did try to manage around any perceived gaps. For example, Robinson felt that there was a shortage of Completer-Finishers in Eastern – 'Often there was no one on the teams to dot the "i"s and cross the "t"s' – and in those situations where he had been the project leader, he had arranged for a professional project manager/administrator to be posted into the team to fill this gap.

In the University of Westminster (and its predecessors), matrix teams have been used for the management and review of subject areas and courses for about 40 years and, in their current form, for about four years. There are multidisciplinary teams ongoing all the time and then *ad hoc* teams set up from time to time to address specific issues. The ongoing teams are the course (project) teams (eg, MA in Human Resource Management), responsible for the day-to-day management of the course which meet once or twice a term. The course review *ad hoc* (project) teams meet to redevelop the courses every three to five years.

Unlike most of the contributors to our research, team members for most of the *ad hoc* teams in the University are largely self-selected. Lecturing staff join the team when they see the need to help solve a particular problem that the project is addressing, and/or to protect their area of teaching, and/or because they want to be involved in the development of a new area or course. Information publicising the setting-up of the project team (eg, to review a particular degree programme) is circulated among the staff currently involved in the subject area and in the School managing the programme. This allows staff to keep an eye on what developments are taking place and how they might be affected. The general intention is to attract a 'critical mass' of opinion-givers or formers. However, with certain projects – for example, the design of the new, full-time MBA – the project team was set up by the Dean of the Faculty of Business, Management and Social Studies (BMSS), who led the project herself. As the first full-time MBA programme this was a prestigious project. The combination of its importance with the fact that a lot of people wanted to be involved, because they wanted to teach on it, meant that the *laissez-faire* approach would have been inappropriate – hence the Dean's inviting staff to join the project team.

Porter commented that there is a feeling in the University that the mixed process (of appointment and choice in team membership) encourages the 'grafters, the movers, shakers and visionaries but leaves out the unmotivated others'. If a key function in the team is left unrepresented by this process, then someone who 'is able and willing to attend' will be co-opted onto the team. Although the Belbin model is taught on the University business courses, there is no use of the Belbin principles or other team-balancing or personality-matching in the team-forming processes in the University. The impression given was that it was difficult enough with the pressure on resources to ensure the system worked at all – there simply was not the time or staff available to take a more sophisticated approach. As we found elsewhere, project teams simply had to manage with the resources they were given.

Although the University of Westminster's approach to the formation and operation of *ad hoc* project teams is fairly common in the university sector, it is in our experience more unusual in other types of organisation, and is possibly linked to the strong culture of academic freedom. It is interesting to speculate what impact the voluntary approach to recruitment has on the success of the project team – whether the team members will be automatically more motivated to the project objectives or to their own agendas!

The LT Strategic HR Unit was comprised of three teams, each with its own team leader. The project leader discusses the selection of the other members of the team with the relevant team leader and, again, selection is based wholly on skills, experience and availability. Although LT generally uses psychometric tests in the selection of stable teams, ie to join the general pool of consultants in the Strategic HR Unit, they are not used to allocate individuals to particular project teams. However, Vessey commented that in one of his projects that had gone particularly well he was teamed up with someone who was a Completer-Finisher. This is Vessey's lowest Belbin category, and he felt the complementary personality characteristics of the Completer-Finisher facilitated the project's meeting its objectives.

In the formation of project teams in Rank Xerox, the primary objective is to achieve the required mix of skills, so balancing the team in Belbin-type terms is not overtly considered. Team members are chosen by their general managers and are usually appointed to represent their team, country, or function. Bater comments that 'Team players are preferred (perhaps our generalists?) and most people are.' According to Bater they try to avoid having too many of the same (perceived) personality types. So there seemed to be an awareness of the advantages of having a balanced team, or perhaps, more strictly speaking, an awareness of the disadvantages of having a dominance of particular personality types.

Reid, our contact at the Association for Project

Management, confirmed that, in his experience of the construction industry, availability and professional function were again the key qualifications for selection onto project teams. The teams would be chosen principally on the basis of the functions that needed to be involved – for example, the need for quantity surveyors or engineers. An added factor could be whether they had worked with the particular client before and demonstrated, in the world of project management, a certain 'chemistry' that the client found helpful. Reid added that 'Sometimes the project leader would appoint an assistant who was good at dealing with the people side of the project – acting as a Belbin-style Team Worker' to compensate for the leader's strong focus on the task, echoing the Eastern Group practice of recognising there were gaps in the team roles and intervening to fill them.

The Belbin approach is not given a high profile in ICL. There is an awareness of the Belbin team roles, but Whitfield of ICL explained that this is implicitly, not formally, taken into account in project team selection. Project team members are yet again selected primarily on the basis of technical skills and, because there can often be a scarcity of some skills, this can limit the choice of who joins which team. Usually selection is carried out by the project leader, who will liaise with home managers and sometimes HR staff in making the selection decisions. For long or large projects (projects can range from six weeks to as many years) a personnel officer/manager is assigned to the project or group of projects. The personnel staff would then be responsible for organising recruitment to the team, usually against a specification agreed with the project leader. For these longer-term projects the recruitment is handled more like the recruitment to a stable team, which in effect they are becoming.

Managing around the gaps in team roles
Our findings on the predominance of the pragmatic approach are perhaps not so surprising in the light of later research by Belbin. He found that the most successful team in his experimental studies, the classic 'mixed' or 'balanced' team, 'did not seem as yet to figure amongst winning teams in the business world' (Belbin, 1993). This may be because the research has

limitations, or perhaps because the longer time-scales of the real world allow people to make adjustments in their team roles which are not possible in the *sudden death* of the business game (which was the vehicle for Belbin's research). However, we would consider a business game – where it often happens that a group of people who have never worked together before are put together to solve a problem or complete a task in a short time-scale – to be very analogous to the project team situation, and hence the balanced team role model might be *even more* appropriate to project teams than to stable ones. The extent to which Belbin's research in the business world included project teams as well as traditional, stable teams is not clear.

There might also be a natural human resistance to selecting the mixed team because of the tendency of people to create groups in their own image (the 'halo and horns' effect in selection). Additionally, there may be some other reason, such as that 'Company selectors ... are often searching for the ideal rounded man *(sic)*' (Belbin, 1981) rather than good material for balanced teams. We found from our discussions with practitioners that there was certainly some evidence for this conclusion.

We believe the usefulness and power of the Belbin model for project team working lies in the concept of managing around the gaps in team roles. Why is this so much more important in project teams than in stable teams? One very clear different requirement between the two at the point of formation is the need to be up and running, ie performing effectively as a team, in a very short time. The stable team may well have been formed over a relatively long period, and there will be a team history of performance which will maintain the team's performance in the short term when someone new is recruited. There will also be established team roles played by the members of the stable team which will have had time to settle down. The gaps in team roles will probably have become very visible, and there will have been moves to cover them. In the newly formed project team there is the likelihood that, unless psychometric tests have been used in the selection process, the gaps will not be evident until that team is well established. The longer the gaps remain undiscovered, the more vulnerable the team will be to having to struggle to meet its targets.

Awareness of the balanced team role concept and knowledge of the preferred role(s) of project team members will give the project leader and the project team a priceless advantage. They will be better able to use team strengths, while team members will also have the opportunity to cover weaknesses in informal team roles with their secondary strengths. Our research showed that some of our practitioners were starting to do this intuitively. Our recommendation is that if it is not possible to select the project team taking into account team roles, then at an early stage in the project team's life it is important to iden- tify the team profile and work with the team to manage the gaps.

Selecting for personal skills and qualities

In addition to selecting for the requisite professional skills and informal team roles, there are certain personal skills and qual- ities that make for effective project team members. May of ICL, when commenting on the specification for effective project team members, stated that:

> The type of person selected for project work needs to be resilient and capable of coping with change; want greater personal independence than those in the traditional, functional role. Because of these required characteristics there needs to be greater care in the selection of project team members.

This choice of resilience and coping with change as a personal characteristic is perhaps not surprising for staff who need to be able to move easily from one project team to another and deal with an often turbulent project environment. The need to be independent reflects the loose teamworking relationships of many project teams. Often members are not working together in the same physical location; they may meet only occasion- ally at project meetings; and contact with the project leader may be similarly infrequent. The project team member may have to be able to work in large part independently. They need to be what Adair (1986) calls 'self-leaders', which means 'not just being a self-starter in terms of motivation and work but someone who can sustain himself (sic)'. The sting in the tail is that people who are good at, and perhaps enjoy, working independently may be less comfortable with teamworking.

(This issue is tackled in Chapter 3, where we discuss the need to establish sound team processes and develop the concept of giving the team ownership of the project.)

We believe that working in project teams requires a higher level of interpersonal skills than more traditional, stable team-working. The reasons for this are that team members need to:

☐ be particularly skilled in handling the occasional requirement to work with people from a wide range of backgrounds (including different nationalities), when status and authority can be ambiguous, and when there may be considerable time pressure

☐ work with the support team members whose links with and commitment to the project may be limited. Often the core project team member will have no, or limited, 'authority' over these support individuals and will need to persuade and motivate them to make their contribution. In effect, the core project team members often have to be mini project leaders in their own right, with all the skills (which we shall set out later) of a project leader.

Two key skills that were particularly highlighted by our research were those of handling conflict and being able to give and receive constructive feedback. Problems need to be resolved quickly in the fast-moving, high-pressured project environment, and the ability to comment on others' performance (see Chapter 4), but without damaging team relationships, is very important.

Another commonly mentioned personal skill was that of time management. A major problem for people working on more than one project – be it one project on top of their routine job, or a case of working on several projects at the same time – is the allocation of time to their different roles and the juggling of priorities. Even with the best of planning something will change – one project may get delayed or work will peak unexpectedly for some team members. Good planning systems should at least identify the implications for individual team members of any changes in a specific project. The difficulty lies in the fact that these planning systems often operate independently, ie they are set up separately for each project. The only way for an individual to work out the implications for his or her own workload is to do it systematically and personally. The LT Strategic HR Unit identified this as an important issue for its staff: there can be up to 100 projects on the go at any one time. At the time of our research the Unit was working towards one overall planning system in which all projects are logged so that the resource implications of all the projects taken together can be assessed.

The key to dealing with overload is its identification in time for action to be taken. Here another key personal skill comes into play: being proactive. It is a much-mentioned required personal skill in many jobs, and Covey (1992) lists it as his first habit of highly effective people. In project team members it is *essential* to be proactive. As a result of the looser style of working, with inevitable less close supervision, the project's success will depend on the individual members' taking owner- ship for their contribution and being proactive in finding solutions to any problems affecting this contribution.

In summary, therefore, you would ideally seek to recruit people to project teams with characteristics of:

- [ ] resilience
- [ ] ability to cope with change
- [ ] independence
- [ ] good interpersonal skills, particularly in the areas of handling conflict and giving and receiving constructive feedback
- [ ] good time management
- [ ] proactivity.

In practice, just as with the informal team roles, the pragmatic constraints of getting the appropriate mix of professional or functional skills for the team at the right time may mean that it is not possible to select against these characteristics. The question then becomes:

- [ ] how to provide team members with some of these skills
- [ ] how to organise and manage project teams to cover the gaps between your ideal project team member and the one who arrives on the team solely because of his or her expertise and availability.

In Chapter 3 we shall set out how you can help the individual develop some of these skills and the team to develop processes to support the remaining gaps.

Strategies for the selection of project team members

1 Draw up a personnel specification for each team member's job, including not only the obvious requirements of experience and qualifications but also the personal skills and qualities of resilience, coping with change, independence, good interpersonal skills, effective time management, and being proactive, and select against this specification.

2 If possible, take informal team roles into account in selecting the project team at the outset:

☐ Identify each individual's informal team role profile using eg the Belbin questionnaire *A Self-Perception Inventory* (Belbin, 1981) or other appropriate psychometric tests.

☐ Aim to cover all the roles, taking into account individuals' primary and secondary strengths.

☐ Try to avoid an overload of a particular team role.

☐ Aim for one or two generalists with strength in several team roles.

3 If you do not take informal roles into account at the team start-up, establish them as soon as possible afterwards in order to manage between the gaps:

☐ Identify team members' individual profiles, as above.

☐ Combine the individual profiles to produce a team profile, which will identify gaps and overloads.

☐ For the gaps, identify which team members have the highest score for those roles; agree with them that they will concentrate on covering those roles; discuss with them how they might do this.

☐ For the overloads, get the team to identify the potential problem of the overload and discuss tactics for dealing with these problems.

> This process can form a very productive session on a team inte-
> gration event (which is discussed in Chapter 3).
>
> 4 Identify strengths and weaknesses in the individual team
> members and establish processes to help the individuals and
> team address the weaknesses (again, see Chapter 3).

The role of the project leader

Before talking about the role of the project leader it is important to recap on the terms we use, and particularly to
distinguish between what we call a project leader and a project
manager. In this book, by *project leader* we mean the person
charged by the organisation with delivering the project objectives. By *project manager* we mean the person appointed to
manage the administrative processes – a particularly important support role on the longer projects, as Roberts of Eastern
Group had identified. In many projects, the project leader will
take on the role of the project manager as well. The terms
project leader and project manager are used interchangeably in
different organisations.

There has been a lot of attention given in the literature to
the role of the 'leader'; what we shall focus on is the difference
between the roles of the leader of a project team and the leader
of a stable team.

Task-focused

In our view, one of the crucial differences between the two
roles derives from the three key performance criteria central to
the management of projects – delivering to the specified
quality standards and finishing on time and within budget.
This places a very clear emphasis on the *task* and requires the
project leader to be highly task-focused, whereas the leader of
the stable team will normally be very focused on his or her
function. Ask any HR manager, for example, to describe his or
her role in a few words and, we would guess, the majority
would say something like 'To manage the HR function.' This
would include not just achieving the task-oriented targets of
the function but also managing the issues around the team
and its individual members. Broadly, being strongly *task-*

focused was how most of the contributors to this book saw the main role of project leaders in their organisations.

According to Robinson, the role of the project leader in Eastern Group is not formally set out – but nonetheless he was absolutely clear in the case he described. He saw himself as having a clear responsibility for reporting progress to the board both orally and through presenting board papers. He saw his key role being to maintain the team's focus on the project objectives, to deliver results, and to manage the quality of the result. Roberts was equally clear. His role as the BPR project leader was quite explicit: to deliver the re-engineering of Eastern Group's activities within the 18-month time-scale allotted. He described himself in psychological terms as a 'deliverer', which he saw as a key competency for project leaders.

In the LT Strategic HR Unit, the unequivocal role of the project leader is to take responsibility and accountability for delivery of the project objectives. He or she takes the agreed targets and objectives for the project and breaks these down for individual members, monitors individual and group progress on the project using computer-produced Gantt charts etc, and produces quarterly reports on the project for the management team. Again, we see the *task* as the primary focus.

Similarly, according to Bater, the role of the project leader in Rank Xerox is to maintain the standards of the project, including delivering the results on time and guiding the team through the process, 'keeping on the route map' of the process. Reid of the APM talked about it being 'to get the job done – task-oriented rather than people- or team-oriented.'

In ICL the emphasis on task is tempered with a strong message about teamworking. Whitfield commented that the role of the project leader (ICL in fact uses the term 'project manager') in ICL has changed over time as the company 'has moved from product sales to delivering business solutions. Previously it was often rather like mechanistically shifting boxes – now it is much more dynamic', requiring the project leader to be very proactive in coping with this dynamism. In Whitfield's summary of the role of the project leader he lists 'team builder/big team player' above 'delivery to time/ spec/budget'. He commented that the second role was the traditional one but, although it was regarded as necessary, by itself it was no longer sufficient for successful delivery of projects. May of ICL supported this view, commenting that in addition to managing the project processes, the role of the project leader is to motivate, lead, and coach the team, and to manage the process of team-building – 'And the good ones do!'

The exception to having a clearly defined role was found under the relatively informal arrangements for managing *ad hoc* projects in the University of Westminster. Here, no common role is defined and, interestingly, the project leader in most projects has no formal authority over, nor responsibility for, the other team members. Clearly, this can cause problems, for example in ensuring that people actually play their full part or even attend the project team meetings. Equally it can mean that those who are most interested in, or affected by, the project are likely to attend and perhaps, thus, maintain high levels of motivation and commitment. Alternatively, within the stable School/Subject Area Teams there is the normal hier-archical structure that one would find elsewhere. Perhaps, in the University, having no formal authority over the *ad hoc* project team members is a feature of operating in a knowledge-worker environment rather than in a traditional industrial environment. There may be valuable lessons to learn here for the future of project teamworking as organisations learn to manage the knowledge workers of the future.

Flexibility

Another aspect of project teamworking which is different from that of more stable teams is the impact of the project life cycle described in Chapter 1 on the role of the project leader. In rela-tion to his experience of projects in ICL, Whitfield commented that as projects progressed through their life cycle – a concept rather like the product life cycle in marketing, that is, start-up, growth, maturity, and wind-down – there was often a need for a different style of project leader for different stages of the project. These different qualities at the different stages could be described as initially someone who is a Shaper, capable of pushing his or her way along; then an Implementer, capable of administering and monitoring progress; and finally the Completer, capable of delivering on time (Belbin, 1993). An

ICL company booklet sets this concept out:

> Projects move through characteristically different phases in their overall life cycle. Particularly in larger projects, these stages may last for significant periods (years in some cases), and/or may repeat. Different types of project manager and different project management skills are needed for these different phases, and most project managers are not equally suited to and/or comfortable with all such phases. Someone good at the start-up of a project may, for example, have difficulty with a long-running roll-out phase. Another phase, found in projects of various types, is when a significant change of direction in a project is required to be introduced.
>
> (ICL, 1995)

In reality, however, the start-up project leader in ICL often saw the project from inception through to completion. However, awareness of the different skill requirements of each stage enables the project leader to consider modifying his or her style accordingly as the project progresses.

In the LT Strategic HR Unit, interestingly, what used to happen was that as the project moved through its stages – of generating ideas about the new policies, implementing the new policies, and, finally, monitoring the implementation of the new policies – the post of the project leader passed from team to team. However, the Unit experienced difficulties with handover of the project to the new project leaders: the project seemed to lose momentum at this critical point. The Unit abandoned this practice in favour of having one leader throughout the life of the project. Just as in ICL, the project leader has to be flexible and be prepared to shift the emphasis of his or her contribution as the project moves through its different phases.

Developing stakeholder relationships

Reid of the APM put yet another slant on the varying role of the project leader, suggesting that the role will vary depending on the nature and purpose of the project:

> For example, in building a hospice the traditional project leader may struggle to take into account decisions which centre on feelings. Alternatively if the project is for MI6 the culture will be one of security.

These are examples of the very diverse customer/clients, key stakeholders that a project leader may have to deal with. We talk about 'getting alongside' stakeholders; Geddes *et al* (1990) talk about 'wiring into' stakeholders. It is all about the project leader being able to develop sound and productive working relationships with the key stakeholders. In Reid's examples above it is about building relationships so that you know what matters to the customer or client – in the case of the hospice project, that patient care and feelings can matter more than the project timetable; in the case of the MI6 project, that security considerations are a very high priority. It is then about being flexible – able to adapt the role to the differing needs of the stakeholders and work with them to deliver the project results.

Reid provided yet another interesting slant on the importance of project team leaders developing good stakeholder relationships. He commented that in his experience of the construction industry it was sometimes the client who decided who was to be the project leader. In Reid's view this does not necessarily mean that the 'best' person for the job in terms of forming productive working relationships within the team is chosen, but that the essential chemistry is in place for managing the most important of stakeholder relationships – that with the client.

This role of developing good working relationships with diverse key stakeholders is often more critical for project leaders than it is for the stable team leaders because:

☐ the project will sit outside the normal organisational structure and there may be few established relationships in place

☐ there may be more external stakeholders involved – for example, the client/customer/sponsor, plus all the functional managers supplying the resources for the project.

This role and the associated competencies is echoed by several of our practitioners. For example, Whitfield of ICL talked about the project leader being 'a big team player', in the sense that he or she had to be able to function effectively in the wider stakeholder teams, for example the customer team. Roberts at

Eastern had to be able to operate effectively with the senior managers of the functional units to secure the release of the 'high-performing specialists' that he needed for the project.

Handling risk and uncertainty

Another feature of a leader's role which is more striking in projects than most stable team environments is the need to handle risk and uncertainty. Almost by definition all projects are unique, and therefore the project team will be covering new ground to some extent. For some projects which involve developing new products, technology, or processes the degree of the unknown and unpredictable can be very high. The project leader has to be resilient to live with the uncertainty and manage the risks.

In summary, we see the role of the stable, functional team leader as being function- or process-focused rather than task-focused. We see the role as being a relatively unchanging one and in particular lacking the noticeable life cycle of a project. We see such a team leader operating within a relatively stable and often quite small network of stakeholders, and in an environment where risk and uncertainty are usually only a part of the job.

In contrast, we see the key features of the role of the project leader as:

- being heavily task-focused
- being subject to change as the project passes through its life cycle
- involving 'getting alongside' a wide range of stakeholders
- responding to the needs of diverse stakeholders
- involving often quite high degrees of risk and uncertainty.

Strategies for clarifying the role of the project leader

Prepare a clear statement of the role of the project leader in conjunction with the key stakeholders which:

- sets out the key responsibilities for achievement of project goals (the *task* focus)

☐ reflects the nature of the project and the stakeholders involved

☐ identifies how the role could change in the different phases of the project life cycle

☐ addresses the levels of risk and uncertainty.

Selecting the right project leader

The project leader plays a vital role in the project: he or she is responsible for the delivery of the project objectives. So how do you go about selecting the *right* person for this critical role?

Situational competence

There is one theme that came through strongly from our research and echoed our own experience: the project leader needs to have knowledge and expertise in the area the team is working on, ie should be what we call *situationally competent*.

Robinson explained that in Eastern Group usually the project leader is selected from the function pushing the process, for example engineering for an engineering project, or the generating business for a generating project. In the example he described, Robinson had been the leader of the team that carried out the research and prepared the tender for the acquisition of a stake in a substantial facility in a Central European country. He believed his appointment stemmed from his experience of, and reputation for, having worked in Central Europe. This was combined with the project being seen as of strategic importance and with his functional role being group strategy adviser. Roberts, our other contact in Eastern Group, believes he was appointed as the project leader for the prestigious BPR exercise because he was deemed to be sufficiently senior and, as a former area/regional manager, had wide general management experience. In itself this could be described as situational competence in general management and the operations of Eastern Group.

In the LT Strategic HR Unit the project leader is appointed by his or her functional team leader on the basis of recognised (situational) skills, experience, and time availability. Account is also taken of people's preferences for the areas in which they want to work.

In Rank Xerox the project leader is nominated by the senior managers involved. The project leader is likely to be someone from an operational background, not from a staff function, unless, for example, the team is working on, say, an HR issue. Although Bater did not specifically make the point, the suggestion was that the selection of project leader would be influenced by situational criteria.

In ICL the project leader is usually selected from within the home business that is promoting or sponsoring the project, and will in all probability be one of their career project managers (whom we would describe as project leaders). If there is no one available with the appropriate experience in the home business, the next choice would be selection from an associated peer business unit and so on, until a suitable career project manager is found. ICL have a process of matching managers to projects. ICL's approach is set out in the company booklet *Project management career stream*:

> In summary, the nature of the project and the requirements on its project manager need to be understood, firstly in terms of the objective requirements associated with the key characteristics of the project and the capabilities required for its management in its current operational state. These then need to be matched against *the skills and experience* [our italics], personal attributes and other factors (eg mobility) of candidates. The profiling of the projects is covered in the *Projects Business Management Framework*, but it must be stressed that the objective is to match the overall requirement profile of the project with overall capability profile of the project manager.
>
> (ICL, 1995)

In many universities the course leader would be the first choice to lead, manage, and facilitate the projects reviewing the courses – the most obviously situationally competent person. For example, in a project to review an existing DMS course, the course leader for the full-time stream was appointed as project leader. In the University of Westminster the head of school generally takes the lead, or even the dean of the faculty herself, depending on the perceived importance of the project. For example, the project team appointed to design the new, full-time MBA was led by the dean.

That the leader should have a specialist expertise depending on the *nature* of the project is an argument also put forward by Roger Leveson and implemented in his own company:

> For instance, a modern head-office complex will entail high specification and design excellence, so we will ask an architect to project manage. Alternatively, in the case of a fast-track retail refurbishment we need to focus on time, so we would appoint a team leader with a programming and planning background. On the other jobs, cost remains the client's primary interest and a quantity surveyor leads the team.
>
> (Leveson, 1996)

In this case project leaders in his company are chosen primarily from the specialism that can demonstrate expertise in the key *performance criterion* which takes precedence.

This view of the need for the leader to be 'situationally competent' is not a new concept. Support for the situational leadership theory was very strong up until the late 1970s to early 1980s and has a strong logical feeling to it. In simple terms the theory suggests that, for example, in a medical situation a team might look to a doctor to provide leadership; in a military situation, to someone with military experience. At its simplest the *situation* was concerned primarily with the task facing the group. Later theories also began to take into account other aspects of the situation, such as the nature of the group and their relationship with their leader.

A major influence on the thinking about leadership came with the publication of John Adair's research and his theory of the 'functional approach to leadership'. Adair argued that the successful leader is less dependent on having the requisite situational knowledge and skills than on his or her ability to keep in balance the key issues of achieving the task, building and maintaining the team, and developing the individual (Adair, 1983). (See Figure 1 for details of Adair's theory.) Adair argues very strongly that the leader who fails to keep the three circles in balance, often through being too task-oriented, will struggle to reach his or her team objectives.

Empowering leadership
We believe that Adair's theory of functional leadership raises some interesting questions and issues about the *leadership of*

Figure 1

THREE INTERLOCKING NEEDS OF TEAM LIFE

The needs of the team can be summarised as follows:

Task   The need to ensure that the required task is continually achieved. The task is usually seen in terms of things rather than people.

Team   The need to develop and maintain teamwork and team spirit among the members so that the team is greater than the sum of its parts and so the task can be effectively accomplished. This need refers primarily to people and their relationships with each other.

Individual Individuals bring their needs with them into the teams. People work in teams not only because of interest in the task to be accomplished but also, for example, because of their need for belonging and for development.

The interrelation of task, team, and individual needs can be depicted as three overlapping circles:

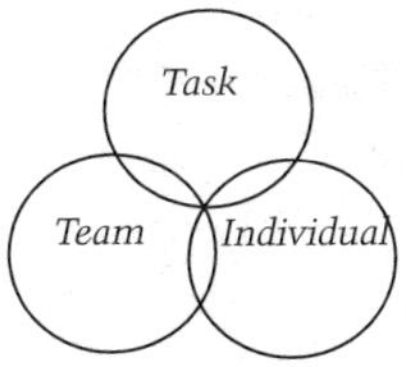

Task

Team *Individual*

If you accomplish the required *task* the effects will flow into the *team* circle and help to create a sense of unity. The effects will also influence the *individual* circle, giving a sense of job satisfaction, and the model will be in balance. If you have good teamwork, you are more likely to accomplish the task, and individuals like to belong to a successful team. If the individuals concerned are fully motivated and involved, then they are going to give much more to the task and to the team.

  Another way to look at the model is as three interconnecting balloons with a fixed supply of air in them. Total concentration by the team leader on the task, while ignoring team and individual needs, would be shown in the model as drawing air pressure from the team and individual balloons. The size of the task balloon is increased at the expense of the team and individual balloons, or both. If this goes on for too long, the team and individual balloons become too small to overlap, signifying a breakdown in the team's ability to tackle the task and the unwillingness of individuals to make the necessary contribution to work as a team in the accomplishment of the task.

  You can work round the model, showing the impact that concentration on maintaining the team as a team regardless of any other issues has on the achievement of the task and on the ability of people to develop as individuals in their own right.

Similarly, if individuals focus solely on their own needs, inflating the individual balloon, they will cease to work as a team, with a resulting difficulty in achieving the task.

This discussion develops in our own words the model described in Adair (1983). A useful brief summary of his views is provided in Adair (1997).

project teams. In the previous section we have stated that the role of the project leader entails being task-focused. According to Adair's theory this would inevitably mean that the project leader would not be devoting sufficient time and energy to the other two circles – building and maintaining the team, and developing the individual. As regards the team, we would argue that project leaders need to accept this outcome and develop a different style of leadership – what we have called *empowering leadership*. In this case we are talking about empowering the team to take ownership for maintaining and building itself. We shall set out how to do this in Chapter 3, but the project leader needs to encourage and support the team in taking on this part of the leader's role. It is not so much abdication as *sharing* the role with the team. As regards the role of developing the individual, once again this may require a different approach. We shall suggest in Chapter 4 that with project teamworking the project leader's role is generally limited to the training and development directly associated with the work of the project. Addressing the longer-term development of the individual will require other strategies.

Project management skills

Another interesting issue is whether the project leader should be qualified in project management skills. ICL was unique in our case-studies in having professional project leaders across the business. The ICL booklet *Project management: career stream* (ICL, 1995) sets out in some detail the generic principal accountabilities for their project managers ('project leaders' in our terms), the capability and experience requirements for different levels of project, and the key personality attributes. Eastern Group does not have career project leaders, except in the information technology (IT) area. However, Robinson of Eastern believed that it would be a good idea if there was such a role – otherwise, inexperienced project leaders have a very steep learning curve in project management skills when first leading a project team. In the LT Strategic HR Unit everyone was trained in the basic skills of planning, monitoring, and controlling projects.

We believe that there are considerable advantages in project leaders being equipped with such skills, but it will depend on the extent to which project working is mainstream to an organisation's activities whether the ICL approach is appropriate. For staff who are only occasionally project leaders, focused training immediately prior to taking on the role may be the best approach. It is salutary to note that the LT approach of training everyone in project management skills at one time suffered from the problem of a fall-off in those skills in staff who did not use them for some time after the training (Farmer and Bee, 1995).

Seniority and authority

Seniority also seems to play an important role in the selection of the project team leader. Roberts in Eastern Group felt that his selection was based not only on his situational competence of a good understanding of Eastern's operations, but also on the fact that he was deemed to be sufficiently senior to handle this high-profile and key BPR project. In Rank Xerox, Bater commented that the hierarchical level of the leader sets the tone for the project – a more senior person being appointed to a more important project, and vice versa. Similarly, in the University of Westminster the most important projects were headed by senior managers in the faculty. In ICL there are 'career streams' or grades for their project managers, based on experience and capability. The reason for this link with seniority is perhaps obvious:

- ☐ Important projects may be deemed to need the experience and expertise of a senior manager.
- ☐ In the context of the project leader's role in dealing with the major stakeholders (the client or customer, resource managers etc) it may be felt that the project leader needs the 'clout' of hierarchical authority.

However, and interestingly, according to Bater the project team leader in Rank Xerox is not necessarily the most senior person involved; that is to say, the team leader may well co-ordinate and lead project team members from a level in the organisational hierarchy higher than his or her own. In the LT Strategic HR Unit this can often be the case as well; for example, projects are usually led by senior HR consultants but the teams may include very senior operational staff, such as the business managers or even general managers of the lines. This is one of the key differences we highlighted between project teams and stable teams in Chapter 1. The fact that a project leader might not always have hierarchical authority suggests the need for strong interpersonal and negotiating skills.

Personal skills

A final issue concerns the particular make-up of project teams. Earlier in this chapter we commented on Belbin's perceived need for Apollo teams (those of the cleverest people) to be carefully balanced in their composition. Belbin had also discussed the personality requirements for the leader of an Apollo team. In commenting on the personality differences between the leader of 'classic' teams and that of Apollo teams, Belbin concluded that 'clever people seemed to need leadership of a different style and type from people who are not so gifted'. In today's language we might identify Belbin's 'clever people' as the highly skilled and competent knowledge workers. So far as the personality of the chairman of successful Apollo teams was concerned, Belbin stated that there was:

> a marked rise in those personality scores suggesting suspicion and scepticism compensated by a small fall in dominance and a move away from the concern for practical matters towards an interest in broad essentials. ... The Apollo CH (Chairman) leader ... is less of a searcher after talent; rather he is a tough discriminating person who can hold his ground in any company; yet he never dominates.
>
> (Belbin, 1981)

Clearly the selection of the project leader with appropriate personality traits is a key issue, particularly when you are putting together an 'Apollo' team. We would suggest that there are parallels between Apollo and many project teams – by this we mean there is the tendency to want to form the project team from the best people. Interestingly, in the professed Apollo team of the BPR project, Roberts was intuitively keen to take an overview and concern himself with the broad essentials rather than the detailed practicalities of managing the project. He compensated for this by appointing a project manager/administrator to deal with the detail.

Table 3

KEY CHARACTERISTICS OF A PROJECT LEADER

Characteristic	Description
Situationally competent	Sufficient knowledge and expertise in the subject area of the project.
Task-focused	Clear focus on project objectives. Sees main responsibility as delivering the project results. Good manager of time and priorities.
Flexible	Able to deal with the requirements of the different phases of the project; and to respond to the differing needs of the key stakeholders.
Networker	Identifies and develops constructive working relationships with all stakeholders.
Empowering leader	Provides the framework and supports the team in managing its own processes.
Process-skilled	Appropriate knowledge and skills for the planning, monitoring, and control of the project.
Overviewer	Concentrates more on the overview than on the day-to-day, delegating the management of routine project processes.
Resilient	Deals well with uncertainty and bounces back from setbacks.
Forceful facilitator	Facilitates the team in managing the project: – but is willing and able to challenge approaches and decisions – is skilled in handling conflict – is skilled in giving and receiving constructive feedback.

Based on the role of the project leader outlined earlier and the selection issues identified so far, Table 3 sets out the key characteristics that differentiate a project leader from a stable team leader.

Perhaps surprisingly, given that recruitment and selection are seen as a major HR activity, we found little involvement of the HR function in the selection of the project leader or project team members generally. Reid of the APM actually stated that in his experience the HR function is not traditionally involved because, in his view:

> People from the HR field do not know sufficient about the wider business activities. They are involved traditionally, however, in determining salary bands, pay and conditions and especially, where there is an overseas element to the project, the ex-patriate arrangements. Otherwise their involvement is usually around the administrative aspects of recruitment – processing the appointment forms after the decisions have been taken.

One suspects that, as with the selection of the general project team members, the pragmatic needs of finding someone with situational competence, of appropriate seniority, *and* who is available limits the choice! However, we would advocate that, granted the key roles played by project leaders, a more systematic process be used for their selection; this could and, we would argue, should involve the skills and experience of the HR professional. Where the choice is limited the use of a systematic process will identify the gaps in competencies which can then be positively addressed through training and coaching etc.

Strategies for selecting a project leader

1 Prepare a written personnel specification for the leader of every project, which takes into account:

☐ the key personal characteristics that distinguish a project leader from a leader of a stable team, as set out in Table 3

☐ the key attributes of the project.

2 Select the project leader against the specification and identify any gaps.

3 Set up appropriate training/coaching/development to fill the gaps.

Handling project team member changes

All teams will undergo changes in their membership over time. However, project teams are distinguished from stable teams by often having a far higher rate of change of personnel. In addition to the usual changes brought about by promotion, departure from the organisation, and illness etc there can be a lot of change due to the nature of project work. Team members may only be partially involved in a project, or be required to play their part at a particular point in the life cycle of the project. It is clear from our experience and our discussions with practitioners that with medium- to long-term projects teams can go through various stages in their life cycle, and different skills can be required of both project leaders and project team members at those different stages. Little attention seems to have been paid in the literature to the issue of coping with changes in team personnel during the life of the project, yet how the change is handled can be very influential on team success. Apollo-type teams in particular, or any other team that feels in any way special (as would appear to be the case with many project teams, for example Roberts' BPR team), can sometimes erect barriers to entry for others who have not yet proved themselves. Also, given the pressure to deliver results to tight time-scales, any new member has to join the team on the run. There is not likely to be the luxury afforded by many stable teams of a gentle period of learning the job.

We suggest that people newly joining any project team after its initial formation require some special attention to help speed their integration. However, the evidence from our practitioners is that generally there is no common approach. Vessey commented that in LT Strategic HR Unit project teams team member changes have sometimes induced tensions within the team when members have been replaced who are perceived by other members to be highly skilled and making a substantial contribution to the project. Vessey also felt that there was insufficient time and attention given to the handover to the incomer, with the resultant effect both on the contribution of that member and on a team's morale and performance.

In ICL members often come into and leave the teams at different stages in the life of the projects. Whitfield distinguishes between the changes which happen:

☐ proactively against a pre-arranged plan
☐ where problems arise and change is needed
☐ reactively to such circumstances as people leaving the organisation etc.

He comments that the more time there is to plan the change, the easier it is for both the individual concerned and the whole team. How new team members are integrated is left to the discretion of the project leaders.

Eastern Group was another organisation where there is really no formal mechanism for making team changes. Robinson commented that, when they did happen, the newcomer is simply introduced to the other team members and briefed by the project leader on the key issues, such as the stage that the project has reached, or their particular role and objectives. In the BPR project, the core team remained stable apart from two changes quite early on, when it was identified that two members were not fitting in or pulling their weight. Roberts took fairly swift action to replace them and said that he felt his intervention had acted as a further fillip to the team's sense of feeling special.

Dealing with team changes was not perceived to be an issue by Bater at Rank Xerox. Their approach (described in more detail in Chapter 3) of training everyone in their quality process oiled, he felt, both the wheels of teams coming together in the first place and any changes thereafter.

At the University of Westminster there is no formal procedure for handling any changes that might be needed in the composition of the project team. In keeping with the informal approach towards *ad hoc* project teams, if existing team members feel no further need to continue their team membership, they quietly drop out with no fuss. If the head of school, the project leader, feels that other people are needed, he invites them to join and they simply come along to the next meeting.

We strongly believe that, in project teams, such changes can benefit from a more proactive approach to ensure that the team that has been put together so carefully continues to

operate with optimum effectiveness. Attention to the selection
of new team members together with a small amount of effort
lubricating the entry of new members to project teams could
pay handsome dividends in terms of the project's results.
Although responsibility for such changes tends to lie with the
project leader, with the more task-focused project leaders a
useful approach would be to empower the project team at the
outset to decide how such changes should be handled and give
the team *ownership* of new team members' integration into
the team. This has the added benefit of encouraging the integration of the new team member.

Strategies for handling project team member changes

1 Plan for the known team member changes – set this out and
let the team know.

2 Decide with the team in advance a process for handling such
changes. Agree:

☐ how recruitment to the team will take place, ideally involving the team in discussion of the personnel specification and
the selection

☐ how any new member will be integrated into the team, what
briefing, coaching or training will be given, and who will give
it.

3 Try to recruit taking into account the balance of the informal
team roles – if this is not possible, identify any gaps or overloads resulting from the change, and work with the team to
cover these.

4 Consider establishing a *buddy* system, with one person nominated as the late joiner's key point of contact.

Conclusion

Putting together the *right* team for the project at the outset is
the first key step on the path towards delivering the *right*
project results on time and within budget. It will not always be
possible to recruit the ideal project leader or set of team

members with the appropriate mix of skills, informal team roles, and personal characteristics that support working in the project team environment. However, the message is: be clear what the ideal is, identify the gaps, and take action to address those gaps.

Now we have the right ingredients, the next step is the *cooking process* to turn those ingredients into a delicious meal. The next chapter looks at how to put in place vital team processes that will enable this disparate group of individuals to start operating as a high-performance team.

3

GETTING THE PROJECT TEAM WORKING

Introduction

We have recruited our project leader and the staff required to tackle the project. This chapter focuses on the challenges involved in turning this collection of individuals into a high-performance project team. Our research identified as the key people challenges the need to:

- [ ] *align* organisational, project, team, and individual objectives – to ensure that the individuals, team, and organisation are working together, focused on the same goal
- [ ] identify all the members of the team – both *visible* and *invisible* – and the contribution they will make to the project
- [ ] establish clear *team processes* – for information flow, managing meetings, problem-solving and decision-making, and monitoring and controlling the project
- [ ] provide team members with the *key skills* needed to work effectively together in a multifunctional, multistatus team.

Aligning objectives

In Chapter 1 we set out as the first phase of any project getting a clear definition of what the project was about and, in particular, establishing the answers to these questions:

- [ ] What are the objectives of the project?
- [ ] What are the outputs?
- [ ] What are the success criteria against which the project will be assessed?

The need for clear objectives, outputs, and success criteria was emphasised repeatedly in our case-studies. It is interesting to reflect whether the extent to which project objectives are clear and aligned differentiates project teamworking from working in stable teams. We think it does. Whitfield of ICL talks about projects having 'single objectives, common purposes' in contrast to 'the multiple and often conflicting objectives' that can beset organisations as a whole. Bater of Rank Xerox, who provided the powerful quotation from St Paul in Chapter 1, explained that the objectives for the reorganisation project were crystal clear (and very challenging!). They were that by 1996:

☐ customer satisfaction was to have increased to 100 per cent (from 91 per cent in 1993)
☐ employees' satisfaction was to exceed the national norm in all 14 countries in which Rank Xerox operates
☐ the return on assets was to be 18 per cent (rising from 7 per cent in 1993).

In the Eastern Group Apple project, too, there was a very clear target for achievement – to reduce the Group's operating costs by £60m (from base of about £180m).

In the other Eastern Group project, the overall objective was again very straightforward – to present the executive board with the necessary information within a specific time-scale in order to make the decision on whether to go forward with the tender bid. Robinson, the project leader, then went on to make explicit what 'the necessary information' was by setting out the structure of the report to go to the board.

Whitfield of ICL listed these statements as his first three keys to successful project management:

☐ 'A holistic view is a prerequisite' – the need to look across the whole life of the project.
☐ 'Be clear where you are going and how arrival will be measured.'
☐ 'Be clear (and remember) why you are doing it.'

Whitfield believes it is essential to understand the demands of the different phases of the project and to be very clear not just about the objectives but how the achievement of those objectives will be measured. He shares our view that you do not have a well-formed objective unless the success criteria are explicit.

The last precept ('Why are you doing it?') is a crucial one. It is about understanding the rationale behind the project – how the project contributes to the organisation's goals. Although projects are set up to be separate, clearly bounded entities, they do not exist in isolation but fit somewhere in the organisational picture. Understanding and communicating the nature of that fit to both the project team and the rest of the organisation can be crucial to the success of the project. Appreciating the project's wider purpose can trigger a real sense of motivation in the team. In addition, the project team will need the help and support of the rest of the organisation – often in the form of information to the team and frequently in the provision of resources. Obtaining that information and those resources will depend on the organisation's perception of the importance and relevance of the project to organisational success.

We see a three-stage process for aligning objectives:

☐ aligning project objectives with organisational objectives
☐ aligning team objectives with project objectives
☐ aligning individual objectives with team/project objectives.

Aligning project objectives with organisational objectives
So how do you do it? In the LT Strategic HR Unit, all projects have a customer – who could be anywhere in LT, eg a manager on one of the business units or a board director. Each project has terms of reference, or a proposal, setting out:

☐ who the customer is
☐ the project purpose
☐ the project approach
☐ the key deliverables, with dates
☐ the resources required.

As well as having a clearly identified customer, all projects must demonstrate a clear link to the overall business strategy for LT. Projects are approved and then monitored by the HR management team.

In ICL, too, all projects have a clearly defined customer, who could be external or internal. There is a clear framework, the Project Management Plan, which is produced at the start of each project and sets out, among other things, the project's scope. This details the specifications, deliverables, and acceptance criteria. Every project is linked back to the line management board. The situation is similar in Eastern Group, where all projects are sponsored by an executive director responsible for presenting papers to the board, including the original terms of reference.

Although the systems are in place to ensure that the project does contribute to the overall objectives – through clear links with the strategic plan (eg in the LT Strategic HR Unit), through clear identification of customers (eg ICL), or through sponsorship by senior managers (eg Eastern) – how well the contribution is understood by the rest of the organisation is less clear. Projects by their very nature lie outside the traditional structures and often outside the normal communication channels. It is very easy for the projects to become divorced from regular organisational life and their relevance to the organisation begin to fade. On the other end of the spectrum, projects can be seen as élitist, absorbing large sums of money and scarce resources for little perceived value.

Robinson of Eastern Group distinguished between two very different styles of project teamworking. The first was characterised by very open and free communication with the rest of the organisation, with the emphasis very much on working with and involving the rest of the organisation. The second style was distinguished by very tight control of the flow of information between the project team and the rest of the organisation, with the emphasis on keeping the project at arm's length from the rest of the organisation. Not surprisingly, perhaps, the second style generated a lot of suspicion outside the project team, although the project was easier to manage. The first style helped relationships outside the project team but, as Robinson put it, the team needed greater clarity of purpose to keep it together, and this posed more of a leadership challenge.

In the LT Strategic HR Unit, although the fit between the project goals and the organisational goals may be well understood within the Unit itself and by senior management, the link may be far less clear elsewhere in the organisation. Members of the Unit are very aware of the need continually to sell the benefits of the project. Where project team members come from outside the Unit they play a particular role as ambassadors, liaising and communicating with their home areas.

So, in summary, the first key steps are to ensure that:

- [ ] the project has clear goals and objectives, and explicit success criteria for their achievement
- [ ] the project goals are aligned with the organisation's goals through, for example, clear links to the business strategy, or through a clear customer focus
- [ ] the project goals and their contribution to the organisational goals are understood not only by those immediately involved with the project but by those in the wider organisation.

The next step is to ensure that the team's objectives align with the project objectives.

Aligning team objectives with project objectives

With the traditional functional or departmental teams there is almost by definition an alignment between team objectives and those of the function or department. As set out in Chapter 1, project teams are different in that often the team members are working together for the first time on a unique piece of work. To begin with, the project team will be a group of individuals – chosen, as discussed in Chapter 2, often for their particular specialism and contribution to the project. For the team member involved in more than one project there will be a strong temptation to restrict his or her interest to that specialist area. As also explained in Chapter 2, Belbin identified a specific team role of Specialist – one who 'provides knowledge and skills in rare supply' but with the allowable weakness of contributing 'on only a narrow front ... [overlooking] the big picture'. It is only too obvious what a team of people all operating in their Specialist roles would be like!

An important role for the project leader is to encourage team members to look beyond the narrow confines of their specialist input and see the team picture through the setting of team objectives aligned to the achievement of the project objectives and personal objectives. Geddes *et al* (1990) talk about the need 'to tease out of the team how the project could be used to achieve some of their personal visions and aspirations'. For example, on a project to redevelop and respecify a major training programme the project team decided to carry out the training needs analysis (TNA) research themselves with coaching and support from ourselves as consultants, rather than by subcontracting the research. This was because the team wanted to use the opportunity provided by the project to develop their own TNA research skills.

The *what* to be achieved is usually set by the project objectives; where the effective and aligned team can make its mark is in *how* the objectives are to be achieved.

Aligning individual objectives with team objectives

We believe that a crucial factor influencing the success of a project is the extent to which the team members, as individuals, feel they are gaining something from working on it, ie meeting their individual objectives. However, it is vital that those individual objectives are aligned with the team/project objectives, otherwise you have the situation so graphically described by Senge (1990):

> In most teams the energies of individual members work at cross purposes... The fundamental characteristic is wasted energy. Individuals may work extraordinarily hard, but their efforts do not efficiently translate into team effort.

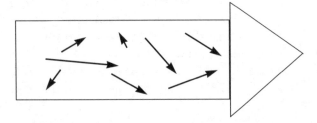

By contrast when a team becomes aligned, a commonality of direction emerges...There is a commonality of purpose, a shared vision, an understanding of how to complement one another's efforts...

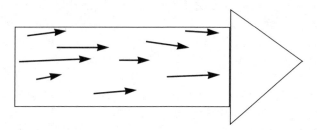

This is a particularly important issue for project teams where members may be only part-time, either because they are working on several projects at once or are dividing their time between the project and their regular job, and so may be juggling with more than one set of objectives – or indeed contending with conflicting objectives. In response to the question 'How are people motivated on project teams?' Whitfield at ICL gave 'aligning the individual objectives with the project objectives for the duration of the project' as the most important factor. Vessey in the LT Strategic HR Unit emphasised, too, the importance of congruency between personal and project objectives: 'People will put more effort into projects that interest them or which they feel will fit in with their career objectives.' The shared vision and complementary efforts (aligned objectives) become an extension of their own visions (individual objectives) rather than an implicit sacrifice of their personal interests to the wider team good.

A common theme in our research was the problems that occurred when individuals' objectives were not aligned with the team or project objectives. Robinson of Eastern Group talked about a particular type of non-alignment – 'turf issues' – that ocurred when team members felt a conflict between the project's objectives and those of their own function. Druker and White (1996) echo this in respect of project teams in the construction industry, commenting that 'reconciling departmental and professional loyalties within crossfunctional project teams is central to the problem of effective performance'. A good example of these turf issues was on a project set up to develop a management information system for an organisation. The project team consisted of staff from all the departments in the organisation that would be using and supplying information to the system. For that project to be successful it was essential that the team members, although they were on the team to represent the needs of their departments, were able to put the project's objectives before their own department's *selfish* needs. The key in this case was the clear vision of how the project's objectives contributed towards the organisation's success as a whole. The team was highly motivated to achieve this vision and was able to sell the proposals to their own departments.

Establishing individuals' objectives is a two-fold process. The first part is to ensure that each project team member has a clear set of objectives reflecting his or her contribution to the project. These will probably be translated into a series of tasks with a timetable for their completion – we shall refer to these as the *task objectives*. These may also include training and development objectives focused directly on the needs of the project – for example, learning how to use project management software, or learning about a specific area of the business.

The second part of the process is the setting of the *personal objectives*, which will be concerned with the longer-term development of the individual. Many of our contributors saw working on the project team as personal development in its own right – maybe in terms of learning to work as part of a multifunctional team, or in terms of the content area of the project, or exposure to and working with senior managers. However, there may be other longer-term development needs totally unrelated to the project that should be considered. Perhaps the individual is working towards professional qualifications, or is hoping to move into his or her first management position. It is important to capture these personal objectives – both those provided by working on the project and those that are separate.

Often a problem occurs because exploring and agreeing the personal objectives will be seen to be outside the scope of the project leader's role, especially if the project has a relatively short time-scale or the individual is working on more than one project. In Chapter 4 we shall discuss the challenges surrounding the setting of these objectives.

The strategies for aligning objectives

1 Establish clear goals and objectives for the project and set out how successful achievement will be measured (ie explicit success criteria).

2 Identify and clearly articulate how the project objectives contribute to organisational objectives.

3 Ensure that the project objectives and their contribution to organisational objectives are understood not only within the project team but also in the wider organisation.

4 Set clear task and personal objectives for individual team members.

5 Encourage project team members to look beyond their specialist areas and build a shared vision embracing their personal objectives and the project objectives.

Identify the 'visible' and 'invisible' team members

Another important difference between working in stable teams and project teams is that stable teams tend to have their own supportive infrastructure. For project teamworking there is what Geddes *et al* (1990) refer to as the *visible* and the *invisible* teams. The visible team consists of those people working directly on the project, ie what we traditionally think of as the project team. The invisible team is all those people who contribute indirectly to the work of the project and the visible team. The co-operation and support of these often *unsung heroes and heroines* is vital to achieving the project objectives. The key is to make sure that while the major focus is on the visible team, the invisible team does not get forgotten.

The first step is to make this group of people visible by identifying them. Take for example a project in which we were involved in the 1980s: the building of a house at the Ideal Home Exhibition by a major building society. The visible project team consisted of members from the housing division (which included the housing and construction arm of the building society), the marketing division (the project was a major marketing initiative), the operational division (who would be responsible for providing the staff to man the house during the exhibition), and the chief general manager's office (because the chief general manager saw this as a project of major significance and was taking a personal interest in it). The invisible team consisted of:

☐ the architectural team responsible for designing the house
☐ the quantity surveying team that did the estimating and costing
☐ the marketing team responsible for all aspects of marketing the house – from advertising and preparing brochures through to arranging press coverage
☐ branch staff who would be manning the exhibition
☐ the construction company that actually built the house (in under two weeks!)
☐ the interior designer (an external consultant) of the house
☐ (behind both these last two invisible team members) a myriad of even more invisible suppliers and subcontractors.

It does not require much mathematical ability to see that the invisible team vastly outnumbered the visible team! This is very often the case. So how do you manage this vast invisible network of internal and external people? The traditional, and in part the right, answer is through the visible project team members. So, for example, the project team member from the housing division would be responsible for liaising with the architects, the quantity surveyors, and construction company. However, a number of problems can arise through relying solely on this approach:

☐ Communication with these invisible team members relies wholly on that particular team member – if he or she either picks up the wrong message or fails to pass on the right one then communication breaks down.
☐ If through pressure of work or other commitments that project team member is unable to manage the invisible team then serious problems can arise, perhaps in the spec-

ification or the timetabling.

☐ If you unexpectedly lose that project member then it can be very difficult to pick up the links with the invisible team members he or she was managing.

As with the project described earlier, usually the success of a project is critically dependent on the performance of the invisible team. The term 'invisible' highlights an important characteristic of this part of the whole team, but because they play such an important role we shall refer to them as the *support* team. There are strong arguments for suggesting that managing the support team should be given as much attention as managing the core project team.

The strategies for managing the support team

1 Identify the support team members at an early stage in the project. Involve the project team – brainstorm:

☐ who they are

☐ the nature and extent of their contribution.

2 With the project team, develop strategies for managing the contributions of the support team members, for example:

☐ via project team members – and if so, decide who, and what their specific role will be

☐ by holding 'larger ' project meetings on an occasional basis involving the support team

☐ via a project newsletter.

Establishing team processes

In Chapter 1 we proposed that a crucial first step for any newly formed project team is to establish how the team will work together – the team processes. Project teams spend a lot of time planning how they are going to achieve the project objectives – breaking down the project into tasks, estimating resources and costs, etc, preparing networks and Gantt charts. All the books on project management devote considerable space to describing how to do this. However, often very little attention is paid to how the team will work as a team. We believe that many project teams underperform because they do not decide at the outset how they are going to work together, rarely review their methods of working, or address the barriers to efficient and effective working.

Yet, in one example of a multifunctional project team – the sports team playing in a match – this concept is well understood and accepted:

> By design and by talent, wrote basketball player Bill Russell of his team the Boston Celtics, we were a team of specialists, and like a team of specialists in any field, our performance depended both on individual excellence and *how well we worked together* [our italics].
>
> (Senge, 1990)

In stable teams, to help the process of settling down, people tend to go through some form of induction process. There is a wide range of literature that describes the need for an induction process for people joining an organisation, and various pieces of research suggest that people who are inducted in an appropriate manner:

- ☐ tend not to drop out early from that organisation
- ☐ tend to become effective in their roles quicker than someone who has not undergone an appropriate form of induction.

If this applies to stable teams then it is likely that it will apply even more to project teams, where often everybody is new to each other *and* where there is the acknowledged need to settle down and start performing quickly. We distinguish between the term *induction*, by which people are introduced to colleagues and the organisational systems of a stable team, and team *integration*, by which people (even though they may have worked together in the past) are introduced to the project team and its specific processes. We also use the term integration to cover the team-building process that we suggest should take place for all newly formed project teams.

In recent years, there has been an increasing realisation of the importance of team-building and development in the traditional functional and departmental teams. There has been a rapid growth in the popularity and take-up of team-building interventions, ranging from informal awaydays, where teams focus on such issues as their vision and values, through to traditional two- or three-day training interventions based around team exercises, to the more adventurous out-of-door approaches. It is perhaps surprising, given the special characteristics of project teams – new teams often made up of people who have never worked together before, their multifunctional make-up, the probable predominance of part-time working, the mix of different grades and status, etc, often combined with the requirement to work against very tight time-scales – that the need for team-building or team integration is less recognised.

Our research showed that focused attention on any form of induction, team integration or team-building, and the establishment of team processes tended to be the exception rather than the norm for project teams. Perhaps because of the very pressure of time that is a feature of project teams, and the short-term lives of some of them, it has not been considered a worthwhile use of time and resources. Vessey from the LT Strategic HR Unit said that there was no common approach in the Unit, but in describing the features of effective and of poorly performing project teams he recalled a very effective one that had held an *awayday* early on. At it, the members discussed their aspirations and what they enjoyed about project working, as well as discussing the nature of the project, and the breakdown and organisation of the work.

There is no standard integration process for teams at the start of projects in ICL. However, when new team members join in mid-project they can be given some form of personal induction. At other times, because of the international nature of ICL's operations, and depending on the nature of the project and the stage that it has reached, there could be wholesale joining by groups of people (including different nationality groups). This can clearly have a big impact on the operation of the project teams and, according to Whitfield, needs to be carefully managed (see Chapter 2). May expressed the view that in ICL some form of team integration or team-building would be carried out by the 'good' project managers, but this was the exception rather than the rule.

Robinson of Eastern Group said that there simply had not been time in his project for a full team-building exercise; team integration was limited to briefing members with a description of the project and their roles. In retrospect he had seen this as a disadvantage in getting the team off to a good start. On other projects there was sometimes informal team-building through social events.

In the University of Westminster Faculty of BMSS, because team members are perceived to be working together on a regular basis there is rarely seen to be any need for a team integration process. Porter reflected ruefully that although they taught their students about the need for and the principles of team-building, they did not actually practise it very much themselves!

Perhaps not surprisingly, given the size and nature of the Eastern Group BPR project, this project team did have a two-day induction/team-building programme. It focused on the objectives of the project, the methodology to be used, and the roles of those involved. In addition examples of successes in business process re-engineering were discussed. Roberts commented: 'There was a gung-ho sensation of the team feeling special at being selected for this important, high-profile project. The programme was instrumental in harnessing this energy and getting the team focused on project objectives.'

In Rank Xerox they take a rather different approach. Every employee receives three days' training in the Rank Xerox quality process. This covers the processes they use in problem-solving and quality improvement, meetings management, and the interpersonal skills required to operate as part of any team. Therefore whenever a project team is formed everyone is familiar with the process that will be used and talks the same 'quality language'. Interestingly, Bater remarked that this even works when the project team, such as the one set up for the benchmarking study, has members from a number of different countries. The company culture of quality teams working on projects transcends national boundaries.

Reid of the APM supported the need for establishing team processes, but pragmatically linked the extent of any event to the length of the project. As he succinctly put it, 'Coffee and a bacon sandwich for a three-week project, a meal out for a three-month project, but a three-day workshop for a large project estimated as taking three years.' Reid felt that these 'partnering' workshops were essential for the success of large projects, and the time spent on team integration was time very well spent.

So what are the team processes that need to be established? The key areas are:

☐ information flow
☐ understanding roles and responsibilities
☐ managing meetings
☐ problem-solving and decision-making
☐ monitoring and controlling the project.

We strongly advocate that there be a team integration event for, among other things, establishing team processes. These will work only if every member is committed to them. Involving the members in setting up the processes will ensure that ownership lies with the team. Also, it is during the period of establishing these processes that the team will start to go through the important development cycle of forming, storming, norming, etc which we set out in Chapter 1. It will be the first crucial step in the team learning to work together.

Information flow

Each project team needs to establish an information strategy. This may sound a rather grand undertaking – surely talking about a strategy is overdoing it a little! We argue an emphatic no – good communication of information is at the heart of successful project management. *Project teams more than any other teams need clear and reliable information channels.* Also, as discussed earlier, projects and their teams often sit outside the normal communication processes – so it is like starting from a greenfield site. There is the opportunity as well as the need to get an information flow process that really meets the requirements of that particular project.

The first step is to complete a communication planning chart identifying the communication needs of all the stakeholders in the project. This is the time when crucial decisions

Table 4
EXTRACT FROM A COMMUNICATION PLANNING CHART

Who needs information?	What is their role?	What information do they need?	Why do they need the information?	When do they need the information?	How do they want to receive it?
Core team member (eg Sarah Jones).	From the marketing dept, responsible for all marketing elements of the project.	Minutes of project meetings.	For information and to take any follow-up action.	Within 48 hours of the meeting.	E-mail.
		Monthly review reports.	For information and to report back to the marketing management team.	By the 5th of the following month.	E-mail.
		Any changes to the specification for the house	Will affect the graphics for the brochures.	Immediately.	By phone, followed up by details through internal post.
Support team members (eg Don Hazell).	From the architect's dept, head of small team designing the house.	Any information that affects the design of the house.	To take action as regards the design and specification of the house.	Within 24 hours of any decision.	Fax to tel no:...
Stakeholders (eg Pat Standish).	Director of housing dept, sponsor of the project.	Monthly review reports.	For information.	Within 48 hours of the meeting.	Internal post.
		Ad hoc reports produced to seek a decision on a major element of the project.	For making a decision.	Within 48 hours of the need for a decision being identified.	Internal post.

are made, eg about how communication with the support team members will take place (directly or through a core member), exactly what information the stakeholders need, and how quickly team members require information. The application of this to our house-building example is set out in Table 4.

Completing the chart in Table 4 thoroughly, considering the needs of *all* the people who will contribute to and have an interest in the project, will ensure that the right information gets through to the right people at the right time. It also sets standards in terms of time-scales for receiving information, which should help to ensure that the communication process is taken seriously.

The second step – the other half of the strategy – is to make clear who is responsible for providing the information. This responsibility may lie with one person – often the project leader or, for large projects, there may be a dedicated project manager/administrator responsible for the administration processes – or it may be shared. The responsibility for achieving the communication standards set out above should then be translated into task objectives for the individual(s) concerned. Meeting these communication objectives should be seen as important as meeting the task objectives directly associated with the project.

Understanding roles and responsibilities
The importance of team members understanding their own and others' roles and responsibilities is well understood in traditional stable departmental teams. Yet again, the special characteristics of project teams puts an added emphasis on this process. Members of project teams (unlike members of most other teams) generally do not have written job descriptions setting out their roles and responsibilities in any detail. These will be determined usually at the planning stage of the project. So the first stage of the process is the agreement of team members' individual task objectives. The next stage is sharing information on these individual task objectives with the whole team. This is usually approached through the preparation and circulation of Gantt charts. (A Gantt chart shows the project broken down into its component tasks in the form of a bar chart with activities/tasks listed on the vertical axis

and time along the horizontal axis. A full description is given in Chapter 4.) However, they are essentially planning and monitoring documents and suffer three major disadvantages as a communication tool for the purpose of understanding other team members' roles and responsibilities:

☐ The degree to which the tasks are broken down may vary – some tasks may be shown only at a very global level, and for those not directly involved in that task may not convey the full picture of the activities that make up that task.

☐ Often the tasks are described in a very abbreviated way and so do not effectively describe the nature of the work involved.

☐ Although they may show the way tasks relate to each other in terms of the sequencing of events, they do not describe specifically how they interrelate; for example, a Gantt chart would not have shown that the marketing team for the Ideal Home project needed to have artist's drawings of the house before the brochure went to print.

We see the need for a process that goes beyond the Gantt chart and provides more detailed role analysis. This would clarify each project team member's roles and responsibilities in respect to every other member of the team. The process would involve each member discussing and negotiating with all the others in turn the way they interface. The process should go beyond discussing simply task-related issues and associated behaviours, and also explore how the relationship works in terms of interpersonal behaviours.

The process will need to reflect the complexity and size of some projects: it may be necessary to break down the project team into subteams around task areas rather than involving the whole project team. Also, the more dynamic nature of the project team – individual members may change, and even the same individual's roles and responsibilities within the project may change over time – means that, for projects with a longer time-scale, the process will need to be repeated at key stages.

The results of these discussions and negotiations can then be formalised by each team member producing a document setting out his or her roles and responsibilities in respect of each other member. In some organisations they have chosen to call these documents Service Level Agreements (SLAs). We refer to them as Individual Service Level Agreements (ISLAs). SLAs are more usually associated with supplier–customer relationships between organisations. However, just as they are intended to capture the service standards expected, so the ISLAs capture the service standards between individuals as internal customers of each others' services.

The process ensures that every team member is clear about:

☐ his or her own roles and responsibilities
☐ the roles and responsibilities of every other team member
☐ who the key team members are who depend on their services, and what specific services (with standards) they need to deliver to them
☐ which team members they depend on, and the level of service they are expecting from them.

Although it takes time, this process should be gone through by *all* project teams. The time required is directly related to the size and complexity of the project: for a small project it can be completed in a couple hours, whereas a large project could take a couple of days. Regard the time as an investment. If team members are really clear about each others' roles and responsibilities, the likelihood of work falling through gaps or any duplication of activities can be dramatically reduced, with significant savings of time and cost overall, and improvements in the quality of the finished product.

Managing meetings

For most project teams *the* major method of intra-team communication is the project team meeting. Depending on the intensity of activity on the project, these may be held daily or as infrequently as once a month. A first key decision for the team will be how often the team needs to meet. However, before they can decide this, they need to agree on the purpose of the meetings. Regular meetings can become tedious rituals and ends in themselves unless they have a clear focus and aims.

There are three main purposes of a meeting, namely, to:

☐ give and receive information

☐ discuss problems and explore solutions

☐ make decisions.

As there are many other ways, often less resource-intensive, for communicating information, we would argue that the primary purpose of project meetings should be the resolution of those problems and the taking of those decisions which would benefit or require inputs from the majority of the project team. The crucial questions are how frequently those key problems are likely to arise and how quickly the team needs to resolve them. Involving team members in the decision on the frequency of the meeting has the two advantages of ensuring that the frequency is appropriate to the needs of the project team as a whole and of helping to gain members' commitment to attending them.

One of the banes of many projects, particularly with large teams of members who perhaps have only a relatively small percentage of their work tied up with a particular project, is getting people to attend project meetings. The great deterrents to attending project meetings are:

☐ seeing no benefits in attending – neither learning from nor contributing anything worthwhile to the meeting

☐ poorly managed meetings so that they take too long, or allow for insufficient discussion on key matters, or where conflict is badly handled.

Although we have suggested that giving and receiving information should not be their main purpose, project meetings are often a convenient method for communicating information relevant to all team members. The key is to ensure that:

☐ the information is relevant to the *whole* team

☐ it is presented effectively and efficiently

☐ the information part of the meeting does not dominate to the detriment of the main purposes of the meeting.

Given that many project teams actually meet face-to-face and work together only at project meetings, these meetings can have an additional powerful role in continuing the process of team integration. When managed well, they can serve a number of underlying processes:

☐ They create identity, cohesion, and a sense of togetherness – meetings help to make the team visible.

☐ They help to make team members feel involved in discussing and arriving at decisions – which in turn produces a sense of ownership and commitment to those decisions.

☐ They develop synergy – the creative energy that helps the team achieve collectively more than individual members could on their own.

☐ They provide an opportunity for teams to celebrate their success together ...

(Geddes *et al*, 1990)

We suggest that project teams use the team integration event, or part of the first project meeting, to discuss a meetings protocol, ie how meetings are to be managed in the future. Suggested issues for inclusion are:

☐ preparing the agenda
☐ chairing the meeting
☐ recording the meeting
☐ ground rules for behaviour at meetings
☐ reviewing the meeting.

Some of the decisions in respect of these issues, together with comments, are set out in the Appendix. There is nothing special or different about the protocol proposed above – it would apply to any team meeting. The difference for project teams lies in the importance of effective meetings to the success of the project. This is because project team meetings:

☐ are often composed of people who work only infrequently together – and hence do not have so much opportunity to build up productive relationships

☐ have to deliver the goods – it is essential that the business is achieved in the time-scale.

A meetings protocol, devised and agreed by the project team at the outset, provides a structure and method of working that helps manage the gap between the ideal of a stable team which has learned to work together over a long period of time to achieve optimum performance and one that is having to learn on-the-job. Getting the processes right at the outset will ensure that those project team meetings are super-productive.

Problem-solving and decision-making

As we stated earlier, one of the main purposes of the project team meeting is to solve problems and take decisions. Commonly problems occur around the three key related aspects of the project: cost, time, and specification. As these are usually targets for the project, problems of running over cost or time, or being unable to meet the specification, mean that the project and the project team often feel under pressure. It is difficult enough for a well-established and stable team to work effectively under pressure; these difficulties are exacerbated for project teams. Senge (1990) describes the issue as:

> The problems compound in a diverse cross-functional team...Each team member carries his or her own, predominantly linear, mental models. Each person's mental model focuses on different parts of the system. Each emphasises different cause–effect chains.

It is vital that the team has appropriate processes in place to help them exploit the advantages of the variety of mental models and cope with the problems that this diversity of thinking processes poses.

Often problems have to be solved and decisions made very quickly, so a first decision area is to set the limits of individual discretion – for the core project team members and in particular the project leader. This is not easy, because the uniqueness of projects often makes it difficult to forecast the types of issue that might come up. Boundaries relating to time and cost variations, eg up to 5 per cent, can be set, but issues around the specification of the project can rarely be decided by individuals alone. The other approach often adopted is to give the project leader the power to decide whether a decision should be taken under delegated authority or referred to the project team as a whole.

As with the approach used by Rank Xerox in their quality training described earlier, it is often helpful to set up a model of how problem-solving will be tackled. We would suggest that there are three principal criteria for effective decision-making in project teamworking, namely that the decision should be:

☐ logically sound (*quality*)
☐ understood and have the commitment of those who are to carry it out (*acceptance*)
☐ taken as quickly as possible (*efficiency*).

Often the emphasis is primarily on the first criterion; however a decision or problem-solution is only as good as its implementation. In project teams where the members will often have to implement their part of the decision on their own, or influence the support team to implement the decision, the second criterion becomes essential. Again in project teams, where there is a heavy emphasis on meeting time targets, the time taken to reach a decision, the third criterion, highlights the need to have an efficient as well as effective process. The advantage of using a model that is understood and agreed by those using it is that:

☐ no time is wasted discussing *how* to solve the problem
☐ as the team becomes experienced in using the model they will get better and quicker in applying it.

Consider, for example, the Ten-Step Model for Problem-Solving in Table 5.

Table 5
TEN-STEP MODEL FOR PROBLEM-SOLVING

I	Clearly define the problem. This is an absolutely key first step: 'The most common mistakes in management decisions is the emphasis on finding the right answer rather than the right question' (Drucker, 1954). Put it in writing – perhaps on a flip-chart – to enforce clarity and definition. It is often helpful to consider breaking the problem down into smaller chunks. A set of problems can get packaged together on the assumption that they are related in some way and have a common solution. It can be worth challenging that assumption. Check that the whole team agrees on the problem definition. (Some teams formalise this by actually signing the relevant flip-chart.)
2	It is vital to be very clear on the outcomes of the problem-solving session. Decide what the objective of this session is. Is it to: ☐ agree a solution ☐ agree a solution and plan its implementation ☐ agree two or three options to be put forward for decision by someone else,

eg the overall steering group for the project, the client/customer?

3   Check that the team has all the resources it needs to meet its objectives. Does it have:

☐ the appropriate people to contribute to the process
☐ enough time
☐ all the relevant information?

If not, what is the best approach? For example, if all the relevant information is not available, can it be obtained within the required constraints of time and cost? What are the risks or problems of proceeding without the information, or with partial information? It is well worth the time to go through this stage. There is nothing worse than attempting to solve the problem and realising half way through the process that it is not possible. Encourage all project team members to contribute to this discussion on resources.

4   Plan the session – how much time is to be allocated to the various stages?

5   Interpret and analyse the facts. There is a range of problem-solving techniques that can be used to analyse the information, eg Strengths/Weaknesses/Opportunities/ Threats (SWOT) analysis, fishbone analysis, or forcefield analysis. Consider setting up training to ensure that all team members are familiar with these techniques and feel very comfortable using them. Positively encourage the use of these sorts of technique, rather than just general discussion.

6   Generate solutions. Encourage people to think widely and creatively for solutions using techniques such as brainstorming. (See useful descriptions in Osborne, 1957, and Young, 1993.) Be disciplined in all such approaches, eg with brainstorming, don't allow people to challenge or comment on the ideas as they are generated. Lay down at the outset the rules of the process to be used.

7   Evaluate the solutions. First agree the criteria against which the solutions are going to be judged (eg cost, time, need for training) and then methodically evaluate each of the solutions against those criteria. Some of the perhaps more unusual solutions may drop out an early stage. However, don't underestimate the value of, or discard too soon, what seem like bizarre solutions – they may actually be the right ones, or spark off a train of thought leading to the right one.

8   *Agree* (one or more) *solutions* depending on your objectives. This may be straightforward in that the *best* solution or solutions are quite clear from the evaluation process of Step 7. However, in the complex world of today this is often not the case – it may come down to judgement. It is at this point that it is important to have agreement on how decisions are to be reached in these situations, eg:

☐ by consensus, ie everyone agrees to support the decision as the best way forward, even though it might not be their own preferred solution. On the positive side this should ensure everyone's commitment, but on the negative side may lead to safe or non-controversial solutions rather than the optimum ones. Also, it can be very time-consuming.
☐ by voting – the solution supported by the majority is chosen. Variations on this can be used; the most sophisticated is probably the single transferable

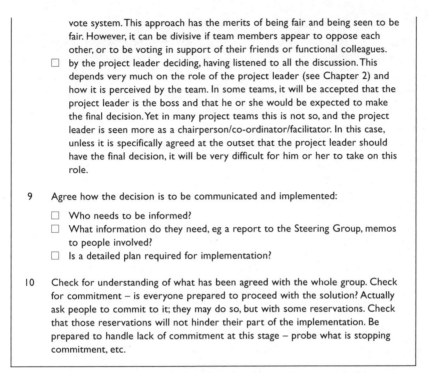

vote system. This approach has the merits of being fair and being seen to be fair. However, it can be divisive if team members appear to oppose each other, or to be voting in support of their friends or functional colleagues.

☐ by the project leader deciding, having listened to all the discussion. This depends very much on the role of the project leader (see Chapter 2) and how it is perceived by the team. In some teams, it will be accepted that the project leader is the boss and that he or she would be expected to make the final decision. Yet in many project teams this is not so, and the project leader is seen more as a chairperson/co-ordinator/facilitator. In this case, unless it is specifically agreed at the outset that the project leader should have the final decision, it will be very difficult for him or her to take on this role.

9   Agree how the decision is to be communicated and implemented:

☐ Who needs to be informed?
☐ What information do they need, eg a report to the Steering Group, memos to people involved?
☐ Is a detailed plan required for implementation?

10   Check for understanding of what has been agreed with the whole group. Check for commitment – is everyone prepared to proceed with the solution? Actually ask people to commit to it; they may do so, but with some reservations. Check that those reservations will not hinder their part of the implementation. Be prepared to handle lack of commitment at this stage – probe what is stopping commitment, etc.

If the team agrees to the Ten-Step Model, or indeed to any appropriate process, it ensures that problem-solving and decision-making are approached in a way that everyone understands and accepts. As the team gets more experienced at working together the process will become second nature. Having a process ensures that the discussion and debate are focused on the real issue of solving the problem, not on how to set about doing it! Just as with the meetings protocol, project teams *need* the discipline of a process more than stable teams: it is another vital plank in getting the project team working effectively in a short space of time.

Monitoring and controlling

We shall talk in detail in Chapter 4 about monitoring and control, and the different approaches that are available. We include a short reference here for the sake of completeness in a chapter dealing with processes. The nature of the process needed will depend on the project, eg to what extent cost or time, or both, need to be tightly controlled, or the tightness of the specification. Often these processes are *imposed* on the project team by (perhaps) the project steering group, the project leader, or simply by there being an established process laid down. An example of the latter approach is provided by the LT Strategic HR Unit. The system there requires that all projects have a Gantt chart which is regularly reviewed and updated. In principle the process is sound, but because some project teams do not see the need for the system as it is, they only go through the motions. The quality of the Gantt chart and its updating then gets increasingly eroded. The moral of this tale is that teams must have ownership of the monitoring and controlling process. This is one of the key team processes that should be agreed at an early stage in the life of a project team, and it should take into account the needs of all the stakeholders (see Chapter 4). It is important that team members are trained in the range of monitoring and controlling processes available, so that they can make informed contributions to the debate of how this process is going to be handled for their project. *The people challenge is to empower the team to monitor and control their own activities.*

Empowerment is at the heart of the strategies for getting the project team working together. In Chapter 2 we made clear that a key personal characteristic of an effective project team member is independence. A project team member can be required to work independently of the rest of the team for substantial periods of time. Yet, at the same time, a cornerstone of project teamworking is the interdependence of team members. The challenge is that people who are good at, and perhaps enjoy, working independently may be less comfortable with interdependent teamworking.

How do you encourage independence without jeopardising team unity? The key lies in the much overused and often misunderstood concept of empowerment. Empowerment is incredibly relevant to project teamworking. In *Thriving on chaos* (Peters, 1987), Tom Peters talks about delegation being the essential prerequisite of empowerment. In project teams, the appropriate skill is to delegate successfully the tasks that make up the project, ie clarifying the degree of authority the person has to act (see Chapter 4 of this book). The most successful project teams are those where each and every member feels a sense of true ownership of his or her delegated tasks – which is given by empowerment. Team members need to feel that they are empowered by the group, in other words *they are empowered to act independently, but that power comes from the team itself.* Hence the importance of establishing sound team processes, and of training and developing people to operate them effectively.

The strategies for establishing team processes

1 Hold an initial team integration event at which team processes can be thrashed out and agreed. The time needed will depend on the size and complexity of the project and hence of the team. Be generous – do give the time that is needed. It will prove a very worthwhile investment.

2 Use the team integration event to:

☐ discuss and agree an information flow strategy

☐ clarify roles and responsibilities, and develop ISLAs

☐ establish a meetings protocol

☐ establish a protocol for solving problems and making decisions

☐ agree a process for monitoring and controlling the project appropriate to all the stakeholders.

3 Use the team integration event to foster the concept of empowerment:

☐ what it means in practice for the way the team and the individual manage their work

☐ what the benefits and possible pitfalls are.

4 Set up arrangements for integrating team members into the team's processes when they join at a later stage of the project.

Getting the team processes established at the outset is like getting the foundations of a building right. If you skimp on the foundations, then you will have a shaky edifice which may stand up for some time but, come a dry summer or gale-force winds, will start to crack. Similarly with project teams: the team may work well to begin with even if they have not established sound team processes at the outset, but when the first major problem or area of conflict arises the cracks will begin to show. We have recently converted a barn to live in. Renovating the foundations seemed to take forever, but then the rest of the work was completed very quickly and the whole project on time. So too with a project team: with good team processes it is likely that the project will be completed efficiently and effectively. The processes form the planks of that bridge between the team that has learned to work together for optimum performance and those teams that are still learning.

Key personal skills for project working

In Chapter 2 we identified the ideal characteristics of people working successfully in project teams. We pick out from there three key skills which are essential for effective teamworking and which can be addressed relatively easily:

□ handling conflict
□ giving and receiving constructive feedback
□ managing your time.

In our view the need for good interpersonal skills is even greater for people working in project teams than for those in stable teams because of the:

□ multifunction, multistatus make-up of project teams
□ need to work with and influence both other project team members and also a wide range of support team members
□ pressure that a project team often works under, which in turn puts pressure on relationships.

The two particular interpersonal skills identified from our experience and research are handling conflict, and giving and receiving constructive feedback.

In project working, with its need for team members to work interdependently while also having to juggle multiple priorities across several projects or several tasks on a single project, managing your time also becomes a key personal skill.

We shall look, in turn, at each of these three key skills.

Handling conflict

Having sound team processes will help to minimise the areas of conflict, but conflict will inevitably still arise. There are many issues in the life of a project that will give rise to differing views and approaches. In a healthy team everyone should feel comfortable about disagreeing with and challenging other members; the difference lies in how this is done. In the mature team, Hardingham and Royal (1994) say, 'the team challenges itself constantly but without emotionally charged conflict'. Guirdham (1990) distinguishes between 'destructive and constructive conflict'. We feel that what differentiates highly effective project teams from the rest lies in how they face up to internal conflict and how the team deals with the defensiveness that invariably surrounds such conflict.

Badly handled conflict can be especially damaging in project teams because it takes up time, which will usually be in short supply, and because it can affect relationships. In more stable teams there are the opportunities and also greater incentives to resolve relationship problems. In project teams both these opportunities and incentives can be lacking: as the team member may not be working regularly with the other party involved there may not the opportunities to *mend fences*, nor the same pressure to do so that arises when you have to work closely with someone over a long period of time. However, poor relationships will affect the way the whole team works together and affect the motivation of those involved.

Druker and White (1996) support our view of the need for 'established ways of working, including ways of reconciling differences and resolving conflict'. The key is to confront the issue in advance, so that the team has the opportunity to discuss how they want to handle conflict and so that individuals have the opportunity to improve their own conflict-handling skills. As part of any team integration or development process we suggest you include a session on handling conflict.

Often at the root of poor relationships and conflict situations lies the inability to give and receive constructive feedback.

Giving and receiving constructive feedback

In another of our books we describe constructive feedback in terms of influencing people at work as:

> perhaps the most important interpersonal skill you can develop. In our view it is the characteristic that differentiates between...people who make effective team performers and those who get in the way of team performance.
>
> (Bee and Bee, 1996)

Constructive feedback will provide project team members with information about their performance and behaviour against their agreed task objectives in such a way that they will maintain a positive attitude toward themselves and their work on the project. It will also encourage them to incorporate this feedback into their personal development plans. In our book *Constructive Feedback* (Bee and Bee (1996))we suggest that in relationships where feedback could and should be a regular feature (for example, between a line manager and a member of staff) a useful approach is to set up what we call a *feedback contract* at the outset. This basically lays down the ground rule that both parties are willing to give and receive feedback from the other. In project teams a useful approach is to set up *team feedback contracts*. This would mean all the team members agreeing that they are willing, and indeed want, to receive feedback on their performance and behaviour so far as it affects the team or the project results, and in return are willing, and want, to give feedback to others. It is vitally important, however, that the feedback is constructive. The skills of giving and receiving feedback can be learned, and a session as part of a team integration/teambuilding event can pay valuable dividends.

Managing your time

The general problems of managing your time in any work situation are exacerbated in a project environment because:

☐ projects usually have very tight deadlines – time is at a premium

☐ project team members may have to juggle with multiple and sometimes conflicting priorities within and across different projects

- there is a strong interdependence between the work of project members – poor time management can affect the work of several other members, and possibly the final outcome for the project.

Sound planning and monitoring and control processes are an essential foundation for good time management by project team members. However, training and development in how to address some of the specific time management challenges of the project management situation can have the double advantage of both improving these skills and focusing team members' attention on them.

The strategies for developing the key personal skills for project working

1 Use the team integration event to explore how team members individually and the team as a whole might handle conflict situations. Cover:

- the differences between the healthy challenging of others' views and conflict

- the costs of unresolved conflict

- models of the way people handle conflict

- a tool to identify individuals' natural behaviour in conflict situations (see Thomas, 1975)

- strategies that the team might like to adopt to diffuse conflict, eg the use of facilitated conciliation sessions.

2 Use the team integration event to introduce the concept of the feedback contract and initiate a culture of team feedback. Incorporate the rules of constructive feedback into the ground rules for project team meetings.

3 Coach team members in the skills of giving and receiving constructive feedback.

4 Provide tailored and focused time management training or coaching to tackle the specific challenges of project working.

Conclusion

In this chapter we suggest that the project team as a whole should be involved and proactive in getting the team working. The first step is the alignment of objectives so that the individual, team, and organisation are working towards a shared vision. The second step is the team discussing and agreeing those key team processes that will define and guide how the team is to work together efficiently and effectively. The final step is ensuring that project team members have the key skills of being able to handle conflict, give and receive constructive feedback, and manage their time. At the heart of this stage of the project team cycle lie the concepts of ownership and empowerment. The project team must own the processes and empower the individuals within the team to play their part. We go on next in Chapter 4 to look at how this strong foundation of aligned objectives, sound team processes, and key personal skills helps to contribute to delivering project results.

4

DELIVERING RESULTS

Introduction

We have completed the phase of the project team cycle –
Getting the Team Working. The team has established its team
processes and, hopefully, completed in large part the forming,
storming, and norming stages, and is now moving into the
performing stage of the team development cycle. The real work
of the project will be underway and members of the team will
be starting to make their presence felt internally and also with
the external stakeholders. In a sense, the team will be in a
honeymoon period, when the excitement of being selected for
this possibly prestigious project is still firing members with
enthusiasm and motivation for their tasks. Bonds will be
forming between them and the hoped-for gelling will be taking
place. All the systems and people will be 'gung-ho', as Roberts
of Eastern Group described the atmosphere in his BPR project
at this stage. So the important questions now are 'How are the
team and the project leader to continue to take things forward,
develop and maintain performance, and keep the project on
track?' 'What in fact are the people challenges of this delivery
phase which, if successfully addressed, will contribute to the
project hitting its target but which, if ignored, will make
achievement of high-quality results very difficult?'

Clearly there can be differences between long projects (for
example those in excess of, say, six months) and short projects,
as we shall explain later, but in our view the key people challenges centre on:

☐ *delivering performance information.* The essential prerequisite for managing individual and team performance is to
have clear, accurate, and timely information on how indi-

viduals and teams are performing. This is particularly important in the context of project teams because of the time pressures and the sometimes loose working arrangements, ie the fact that team members work separately for a lot of their time. There are well-developed approaches for monitoring and controlling projects. However, the emphasis has traditionally been on the tools and techniques – we look at the human perspective of using these tools and techniques to deliver the project results.

☐ *managing individual and team performance.* How do you ensure that individuals and the team as a whole meet their objectives and the project remains on track? The key elements are:

   ☐ clear delegation of tasks – setting up the delegation contract with specific and measurable objectives

   ☐ accurate and timely information on performance against those objectives (discussed above)

   ☐ taking timely and effective action based on this information – probably the element that presents the greatest people challenge, involving the skills of constructive feedback and problem-solving.

☐ *handling variances in performance.* We have purposely used the language of traditional project management, which focuses on identifying and analysing variances in time and costs etc. Traditional personnel language talks about handling non-performance, or disciplinary issues. We like the term 'variance' because of its neutrality – it does not imply personal failure but suggests that there is a difference from plan in performance that needs to be tackled. It can happen! Even in the best of teams some people will perform differently from expectation. There can be a multitude of reasons this should be so. The usual problems that can occur in stable teams – for example, lack of appropriate competencies, failure to use the agreed team processes correctly, or just simply bad behaviour – can be compounded by the particular circumstances of project working, such as problems of juggling priorities across different projects, lack of close supervision etc. There is also the happier situation when performance exceeds expectation, and the question how such superior performance is recognised. The people challenge is how to handle these variances in performance in the project environment.

☐ *training and development of project team members.* Ensuring project team members' skills and knowledge continue to match the needs of the project throughout the stages of the project life cycle is clearly an important aspect of managing performance. However, equally important is the continuing personal and professional development of team members. This can be an integral part of motivation, as it makes a statement that the individual and the organisation have a joint commitment to the future *which lies beyond the end of the current project.*

☐ *motivating the individual and the team.* On the long-haul projects in particular there will be a need to maintain the high levels of performance required to meet the time, quality, and cost targets and, when there are factors adversely affecting motivation, to overcome them. Keeping the team motivated through periods of intense pressure and through the ups and downs of events not going according to plan is another key people challenge.

☐ *rewarding the individual and the team.* Absolutely central to people's motivation is their sense of feeling appropriately rewarded for what they have contributed in terms of commitment and effort to the project, as well as what they have achieved by way of their tasks. This is a complex area in general but can be brought into sharp relief with project working.

An important issue for project teams throughout all these challenges is the question *who* is responsible for dealing with them? For example, who is responsible for continuing personal development – the project leader or the home manager? To what extent can the responsibilities be shared between the two bosses? To what extent can the team as a whole take responsibility for some of them, for example, motivation or deciding on the allocation of financial rewards, so far as these exist? Or what about individual team members themselves – in the dynamic and independent environment of project work, to what extent are their own performance, motivation, and development too important to leave to others and, therefore, a key *personal* responsibility? We shall comment on these and other issues in this chapter and suggest strategies for dealing with them.

There are no clear boundaries between the people challenges of performance management, handling variances in performance, motivation, reward, continuing development etc. They are all inextricably linked and therefore there will inevitably be some overlap as we discuss them.

Delivering performance information

In traditional books on project management the emphasis in this phase of the project cycle is on monitoring and controlling the project. The traditional texts devote considerable space to describing how to monitor the project against the three key criteria of specification, time, and money. The heart of any monitoring and control system is to deliver performance information. It is not the purpose of this book to go into detail on subjects such as cumulative costs curves, variance analysis, and resource loading (to name but a few!) – there are many texts that will do this for you (see Lockyer, 1984; Rosenau, 1992). We shall set out the basic principles but focus on the people challenges presented by this crucial activity of delivering performance information. Our message is quite simple: the strategies for success centre on ownership and empowerment.

Revisiting the planning process

The foundation of any monitoring and control system is the project plan. In Chapter 3 we introduced the concept of breaking down the project into its separate activities and portraying the timetable for these activities in the form of a chart – the Gantt chart. This is probably the most common method of presenting project plans. There are, however, three processes that lie behind the Gantt charts of all but the simplest projects:

☐ The work breakdown structure (WBS) is a top-down approach of generating all the tasks associated with a project. The project is first broken down into its main areas, and then each area is broken down again, and so on. Figure

☐ estimate, as accurately as possible, the time needed for each task

☐ identify and estimate, as accurately as possible, the resources required for each task.

Figure 4

GANTT CHART – PLAN

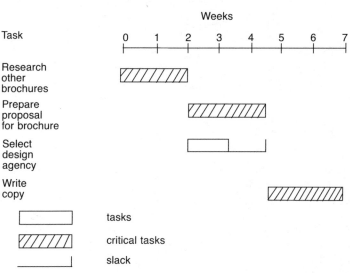

The *how* to do it lies in harnessing the knowledge, skills, and energies of the whole project team – both core and support elements. This is the people challenge of the planning stage.

Strategies for the planning process

1 Give the project team ownership of the project plan. Emphasise that it will be based on *their* inputs – but let them know if there are any constraints.

2 Use the project team meetings to generate the plan. Encourage the use of brainstorming to generate all the tasks. (This can be a valuable exercise for the team integration event set out in Chapter 3.) Encourage team members to go outside their functional boxes in putting forward and challenging the tasks to be included. Do likewise to establish the links.

3 Estimating time and resources for individual tasks can be a time-consuming and painstaking process. Often it will best be done by the individual team members responsible for a task going away and consulting their functional colleagues or support team members. However, the project team as a whole can play a crucial part in this process. Ask each team member to present his or her estimates at a project team meeting and encourage the team to challenge those estimates. This can be a sensitive procedure: it will need all those interpersonal and team skills discussed in Chapter 3 for this to work well. However, the outcome should be both better estimates, a greater understanding by the whole team of the issues involved, and perhaps most important of all a sense of ownership by the whole team of all parts of the plan.

4 Prepare a strong visual image of the plan. Although most of the detailed analysis and drawing of the plan will be done these days by computer (and the master plan will be held on the computer), consider preparing large-scale versions of the project network, Gantt chart, and any other relevant charts for display at project meetings. An interesting point raised by Vessey and others in the LT Strategic HR Unit was that although their system was computerised and was intended to be as paperless as possible, there was a need for these visual images as a focus for the project team.

We believe that giving the individual team members and the project team as a whole a strong sense of ownership of the plan is one of the most important contributions to the success of the project. It is the essential prerequisite for the effective monitoring and control of the project.

Towards team control

First, a few words about the tools and techniques for monitoring and controlling projects. The basic principle is that at regular intervals – the interval depending usually on the duration of the project and intensity of activity at a particular time – actual performance is measured against the plan in terms of the timing and resources used. A common interval is monthly, but it can be as often as daily as the project draws to its conclusion.

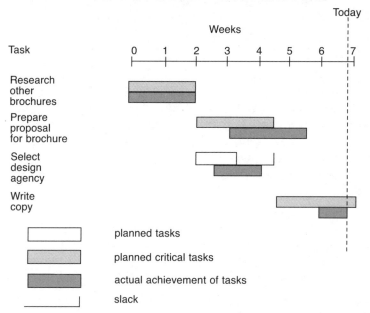

Figure 5

GANTT CHART – PLAN *V* ACTUAL

A typical way to display the performance information on timing is shown in Figure 5 – on the Gantt chart the actual timing of an activity is shown under the planned timing, from which it can be seen whether the task started on time, was of the expected duration, and whether it finished on time. The use of CPA allows the implications for the project completion date of any delays in individual tasks to be calculated. This is usually the key item of information of interest. On larger projects there are often milestones along the way, and the impact of delays on the achievement of these milestones will be of equal if not greater importance than their impact on the final completion date. For example, on a project to implement a management information system, an important milestone would be agreement on the specification of the scheme. Dependent on this date would be the need for specialist computer-programming staff to be available, and perhaps the opportunity to secure a particular discount on the computer hardware required. In one project we managed – involving a large organisation moving offices – a milestone that caused particular difficulty was the type of new furniture to be used throughout the new offices. The chief executive was the person with the authority to make the decision, but – despite several reminders that he was *on the critical path* – his indecisiveness led to the date for the whole move being delayed.

The monitoring of the budget is slightly more complex, but again the basic measure of interest is the difference between the actual and the planned costs – normally referred to as the cost variance. This is usually expressed as a percentage of the planned costs. For example, the project could be 4 per cent overspent during May; additionally, the cumulative effects of over- or under-spending will be monitored, so that by the end of May (which is six months into the project) the project might be 6 per cent overspent. Analysing the cost variances can be quite complex, as it involves the extent to which these are caused by changes in the scheduling of the project or differences in the actual against the planned costs for specific tasks. Understanding the cost variance is important for predicting what the final cost of the project might be.

The key steps in successful monitoring and control are to decide at the outset :

- [ ] what performance indicators are going to be measured
- [ ] how frequently the project will be monitored (this could vary over the life of the project)
- [ ] how and when the necessary information is going to be collected
- [ ] how the information will be presented to the project team
- [ ] how the information will be presented to the managing team/sponsor/client and other relevant stakeholders.

Again, the people challenge is to get the team to take ownership of the monitoring and control process.

Strategies for developing team control

1 State at the outset that, as ownership for the success of the project lies with the project team, then it makes sense for the team to decide on the most appropriate monitoring and control process. Many such processes are imposed following standard approaches laid down by the organisation or the managing

team/customer/sponsor. Consider bucking the first if it does not match your project requirements! Clearly the major stakeholders may also want a say in the process. Encourage the team to decide how they and the major stakeholders can work together to establish a process that will deliver the results.

2 Ensure that team members are comfortable with the various approaches to monitoring and controlling projects. Consider setting up a training session, perhaps led by a team member who is experienced in project working.

3 Use the team integration event (discussed in Chapter 3) or an early project team meeting to discuss and agree the monitoring and control process for the project. Start by agreeing the purpose and objectives of the process for all the stakeholders. This is a vital step. All proposals for monitoring and control should then be assessed against these objectives. Many monitoring and control systems seem to be ends in themselves, and a lot of energy and resources are devoted to fuelling these systems without clear benefits for the project as a whole!

4 Having agreed the overall process, propose that the individual team members assess the implications of the process for themselves, for example in supplying information, and analysing and updating the plans. Commitments to playing their part in the process would be encapsulated in their ISLAs (see Chapter 3) and individual task objectives for the project. Sometimes one of the most difficult and frustrating aspects of project working lies in ensuring that the monitoring and control systems function properly. Information that is inadequate, inaccurate, or received late emasculates the system. It is important that individual team members commit themselves to playing their part.

5 Encourage honesty. As Whitfield of ICL put it: 'Be honest – it [giving bad news on performance] is only painful in the short term.' Often projects get into serious difficulties because problems are not identified until too late. There must be a commitment to share them as early as possible. They should be viewed as opportunities for the project team to display its problem-solving skills, rather than be hidden or ignored.

6 Empower the team to control the project themselves – this is what we call *team control*.

There is an analogy here with the areas of quality control and health and safety. Organisations that have been successful in implementing quality and health and safety processes are those which have been able to make each individual his or her own quality controller or safety officer. *The people challenge is to make each project team member his or her own project controller.*

Managing individual and team performance

This is not a book about performance management *per se* – there are many of these available – but one in which we set out to highlight the challenges of managing performance that are peculiar to project teams and different from those of traditional stable teams. Many would say that performance management is of equal interest and importance to both team environments. We believe that the effective management of performance in project teams is even more crucial because:

- □ there is usually a very clear outcome for a project
- □ there is often a very public focus on delivering results – non-delivery can be an embarrassing and career limiting experience!
- □ there are usually tight deadlines, which means that there is little room for things to go wrong
- □ there are strong interdependencies between the activities of the individual team members – a lack of performance by one member can affect the work of many others
- □ the project is often set up to address matters of great significance to the organisation – for example, Roberts' BPR project for Eastern Group.

Delegating and setting objectives

In a way, the very special aspect of having a clear outcome for projects means that the project team is off to a good start when compared with many stable teams, in so far as it knows clearly what it is to achieve. The WBS process described above then allows the overall project goal to be broken down into detailed tasks and hence the task objectives described in Chapter 3 to be identified for individual team members. It is vital that these individual team objectives are discussed and agreed with the individual concerned. A key role of the project leader will be to initiate and handle these discussions, ensuring that the task objectives are clear and achievable. If the tasks have a long time-scale it may be appropriate to set milestones along the way. The discussion should include, where appropriate, the objectives that the individual has been set in other areas, eg for other projects, to ensure there is no conflict in terms of delivering against all the objectives. A three-way discussion involving the project leader, the individual, and the individual's home manager is often useful at this point.

So we are now well on our way to meeting the first key element for performance management: setting clear and measurable objectives for team members. However, we are not quite there. In our experience, many projects encounter problems because although the tasks themselves may be clearly identified, the task objectives are not expressed in clear and unambiguous terms. McMaster (1986) comments that individual task requirements expressed in vague or woolly terms (what he calls low-quality language) 'will introduce ambiguity, uncertainty and misdirection'.

The challenge is to ensure that every individual's task objectives meet the criterion of a modified form of the SMART model, ie the tasks should be described in terms that are:

☐ *Specific – what* specifically the individual is expected to achieve, and *why*, eg

> Prepare the proposal report seeking agreement for advertising expenditure so that it can be presented at the May Steering Group Meeting.

Possibly you might even describe *how* the task is to be carried out, and *why* in that way, if the person to whom the task is assigned or delegated is relatively inexperienced or unqualified in the work, eg

> Prepare the proposal report seeking agreement for advertising expenditure in *the format set out in the Project Guidelines*, so that it can be presented at the May Steering Group Meeting.

☐ *Measurable* – in terms of time, cost, or some other quanti-fier, or alternatively what you will see, feel, or hear that is different when the task is completed. We are talking about setting clear success criteria for each task.

☐ *Agreed with*, not imposed on, the individual project team members, and involving the other stakeholders as required.

☐ *Realistic* and achievable, yet challenging and stretching – ie tasks that lie within the skills and knowledge of the project team member but which encourage the individual to push against the frontiers of his or her knowledge and skills. They should be realistic when set in the context of the resources that are allocated or can be otherwise obtained and of the individual's workload on other tasks or projects.

☐ *Time-bounded* in some way, either by a specific clock time, a particular date, or by dependency on other events, eg 'Prepare the minutes within four days of the meeting.' The planning process described in the first section of this chapter is aimed specifically at identifying clear time boundaries. Time-bounding can be for the completion of the whole task or for any milestone along the way. For complex or lengthy tasks the use of milestones can be particularly helpful in managing performance. Milestones can be important too for stimulation and motivation: Whitfield of ICL talked of project teams being 'motivated by milestones sufficiently close to give urgency, yet sufficiently far to give an horizon'.

The WBS process is also excellent for demonstrating how indi-vidual tasks contribute to the completion of the project, so individual team members can easily see where their contribu-tion, their piece of the jigsaw, fits into the overall picture.

Setting SMART objectives is a crucial part of the 'delegation contract' – the contract that exists between the delegator and the delegatee to perform a given task to a particular standard by a certain time, ie to meet the task objectives. The delega-tee's side of the contract is to do that which is required to meet the agreed standard. The delegator's part of the contract is to provide support, both material and psychological, and to manage the overall environment in such a way as to make possible the achievement of the task to the agreed standards.

The term *contract* is very important: it implies agreement by both sides to *all* the terms and conditions. It also encapsulates the concept of negotiation to get to that agreement.

Two issues are raised at this point:

☐ Who is the delegator? Traditionally, in stable teams, it would be the team leader. In some project teams this role would be fulfilled by the project leader. However, a feature of many project teams is that the project leader has no hierarchical status but is someone whose role is more that of a facilitator. We believe that if the project team has ownership of the project, then logically the project team should be the delegator. This is what we mean in Chapter 3 when we talk about team members being *empowered by the team*.

☐ What level of delegation is being agreed? Delegation can be given in what we call the 'A', 'B' and 'C' of delegation:

  ☐ *A*way you go and do it (whatever has been agreed) – and I don't want to hear anything about it again.

  ☐ *B*ack to me to report that you have completed the task or, by exception, that you have not completed the task as agreed.

  ☐ *C*lear with me (the delegator) how you are going to do the task before you carry it out.

In stable teams all three types of delegation are likely to be taking place, reflecting a combination of the importance of the task and the degree of trust between delegator and delegatee. In project teams, most of the delegation contracts are of type B, reflecting the trust that team members have not only the required knowledge and skills (usually the basis of their selection) but also commitment to achieve their tasks. Agreeing milestones along the way does not indicate a lack of trust or confidence in the ability of a team member but, we argue, is part of the support that the project team/leader offers the people on the team. The monitoring and control process will have set out how the reporting back will take place. There will occasionally be tasks that by their nature are either so important or difficult that a type-C delegation may be appropriate. For example, if a task in a change project is to carry out focus group meetings with staff, then it may be appropriate for the team member to whom that task has been delegated to discuss and clear with the delegator – the project team – how those focus group meetings will be run.

A clear delegation contract is important in all delegation situations; however, the need is intensified in project working where many team members may be working independently for large parts of the time.

Taking action

We have now completed the first key element for successfully managing performance: clear and agreed individual task objectives. The second element (receiving accurate and timely information on performance against those objectives) has been addressed in the first section of this chapter. This leads us on to perhaps the most challenging element: taking timely and effective action based on this information to keep the project on target. It is here that we find perhaps one of the most striking differences between project teams and stable teams. With an effective monitoring and control system which is delivering accurate and timely performance information, team members' performance (or non-performance) on their individual tasks will be highly visible to the whole team. Also, individuals' work will often be critically dependent on the performance of other team members in terms of the time-scale, etc. In fact the focus of project team meetings will be on the progress to date of the project, and part of the purpose of the meeting will be to deal with variances in performance. In traditional teams, variances in performance are often not so starkly and publicly displayed; they may well remain a matter between the team leader and the individual alone.

This particular aspect of project teamworking can have advantages but at the same time pose some serious challenges. The advantages are that:

- variances in performance are identified and there is the opportunity to deal with them quickly
- the whole team is involved in finding solutions to the problem, which can improve the quality of the solutions and their implementation
- the whole team being involved can be a powerful motivator

to individuals to meet their targets and not let the team down.

The challenges are to handle variances in performance in such a way as to:

☐ encourage team members to be honest and report problems as soon as they occur

☐ constructively deal with the variance in performance by concentrating on finding solutions rather than allocating blame

☐ ensure relationships among the team are not adversely affected.

In Chapter 3 we discussed the need for team members to be skilled in giving and receiving constructive feedback. Not only are these skills of value in the normal everyday working of project teams, but they are also essential when dealing with what is effectively the managing of peer team members' performance.

Here again we see the team as a whole continuing to play a powerful role in the monitoring and control of the project – continuing the *team control* of the project.

Resolving conflicting priorities

Another clear difference in performance management between working in a project team in a matrix organisation and working in a stable team can be seen in two interrelated issues:

☐ Team members may be working on different projects, which could lead to conflicting priorities.

☐ There could be conflicting priorities between the various bosses – the project leaders and the home managers.

Neither of these is likely to arise where someone is allocated full-time to a lengthy project. In any case, in this type of situation it is clearly the project leader's role to resolve any such conflict. Whitfield of ICL confirmed that on their large, long-term projects 'stability of membership can be as great as in a business unit.' Therefore the concept of conflicting priorities did not arise. Hence any problems of prioritising that do occur are likely to arise on small projects, where team members are working on more than one project (or have several short commitments to various lengthy ones) or where the project element of the person's total work is relatively small.

This is not to say that there are not conflicts in priorities within stable teams; there are. The difference between project teams and stable teams lies in the resolution of these conflicts. In the stable functional team 'roles are structured so that individuals can usually resolve conflicting demands by talking to their own functional boss' (Davis and Lawrence, 1977). In a project team comprising people from several different functions the conflicting priorities usually have to be resolved without a common boss to arbitrate. ICL employs an alternative to the common boss in that they use what they call a 'reviewing manager' if the project leader and the home managers involved are unable to resolve any disagreements between them. We believe that it is important that the process for settling disagreements on priorities and other issues be agreed at the outset of the project or as soon as the team member is recruited into the team. Reid of the APM suggested that the ideal would be for the project leader to meet with the home managers at the time the project team is formed and negotiate a charter for the resolution of any disputes between the team members' various bosses.

Strategies for successful management of performance for the project

1 Ensure that all team members have clear delegation contracts incorporating SMART objectives. These should be agreed between the individual team members, their project leader and, where relevant, their home managers.

2 Ensure that project team members handle constructively the discussion at project team meetings on variances in performance of other team members. In Chapter 3 we proposed that rules associated with giving and receiving constructive feedback be incorporated into the ground rules for project team meetings, and that team members receive training and development in these skills.

3 At the outset of the project, or when the individual first joins the team, set up SLAs to handle issues of release, handling conflict over priorities etc. These would be tripartite agreements between:

☐ the individual team member

☐ his or her functional or home manager

☐ the project leader.

So far we have dealt with managing performance from the perspective of keeping the project on track. This is clearly just one side of the performance management story; the other lies in managing performance for the benefit and development of the individual. There are two areas to be explored:

☐ managing individual performance on a day-by-day basis to ensure the project targets are met

☐ managing individual performance for the development of the individual.

We shall cover the former in the next section; the latter is covered in the section entitled *Training and development of project team members* (see page 107 ff).

Handling variances in performance

In the earlier section we described how the project team would have the role of finding solutions for variances in performance that are affecting the delivery of results on the project. Their role does not however usually extend to:

☐ analysing why the problem occurred (only in as much as it may affect the solution) and helping the individual learn from the experience

☐ dealing with issues that may not be directly task-related – for example, behaviour affecting team relationships or the functioning of project team meetings.

In the traditional stable team this is normally the role of an individual's team leader or functional manager. However, the same issue of having several bosses raised in the previous section also affects this aspect of performance management.

There is a real danger that issues are not taken up and addressed but *fall between two stools*: they may be seen neither as the responsibility of the project leader nor of the home manager. The project leader will be focused on finding solutions and moving the project forward (the task focus in Adair's theory) and the home manager may not know about the problems or not feel that it is his or her responsibility.

Interestingly, the contributors to our research (with the exception of Roberts of Eastern Group, who identified potentially poor performance at team start-up and dealt with it by returning two of the initial team to their home functions) did not offer any examples of where performance on a project team had given real cause for concern. This could be perhaps a testimony to the quality of the selection of project team members; or, as was hinted by some of our practitioners, performance might not always be an issue that is faced up to, ie there was a degree of avoidance. Our research discovered that:

☐ in the LT Strategic HR Unit indiscipline 'had not been an issue, so far'. The Unit has a system of *coaches* (see later section) and it would be their role to take up this type of performance issues. However, Vessey indicated that sometimes the coaches 'saw their role as supporting the person rather than the project', and they did not have a formal role in the disciplinary process. Vessey also made the interesting point that some people showed less commitment to projects that did not interest them (recalling the importance of aligning personal objectives with project objectives discussed in Chapter 3); he went on to say that the combination of a rather democratic culture with the project culture could allow 'people to opt out and get away with it' if the situation was not addressed. If there was a serious issue of indiscipline or low performance, a senior manager with appropriate authority under the LT disciplinary procedure would hold a hearing and decide on the outcome.

☐ In Rank Xerox there were no examples of serious performance or disciplinary issues. Bater commented 'the [company] style is not to be too confrontational. They [disciplinary issues] are handled quietly.' In the event that serious disciplinary issues did arise, they would be dealt with by the senior line or functional manager.

☐ In ICL, disciplinary action will be taken, if necessary, 'by the project leader in the project environment, otherwise by the home manager, especially if there is a number of verbal warnings on different projects.' The disciplinary process was, however, rarely used.

☐ In Eastern Group, Robinson said that if the unacceptable behaviour arose in a team situation then the project leader would be the person to take action. If the project team member is just not up to scratch 'they are quietly dropped off the team. Generally there is a degree of avoidance [of non-performance issues]; everything is fairly informal.' Any serious disciplinary issues would be handed over to the home manager for action. On Roberts' BPR project, after the initial problems 'there were no disciplinary issues to be dealt with – people behaved with distinction.' As the line manager to those assigned to the project, Roberts would have dealt with any disciplinary issues himself where the issue related to work on the project; otherwise they would be dealt with by the home manager. Interestingly, Roberts introduced to his team the additional concept of key performance areas (KPAs), centring largely on *soft*, subjective issues which were as much about relationship-building and consultancy issues with the stakeholders as about deliverables.

☐ In the University of Westminster *ad hoc* project teams, there is no formal concept of appraisal of individuals against project objectives, and disciplinary issues 'hardly ever arise'. If they should arise, then the head of school is the line manager for the purpose of the disciplinary process.

In terms of what sanctions might be applied to low performers on project teams (other than being 'quietly dropped off the team'), people in both ICL and Rank Xerox who had failed to perform might not be asked to join further project teams and this, according to May of ICL, 'would be seen as a loss to them'.

Possibly it is because people working on projects are usually chosen especially for that project on account of their particular skills and experience and often on account of their reputation for delivering results that non-performance is rarely a major issue. However, in our experience there can be many examples of variances in performance and behaviour that are not sufficiently serious to invoke the sanction of moving someone off the project team but do nonetheless hamper the delivery of results on the project. Not only can it be frustrating for the project team to have to put up with such non-performers, it is unfair on the individuals concerned to miss out on the coaching and counselling that might improve their performance.

Strategies to address the people challenge of variances in performance

1 In the previous section we proposed the setting up of SLAs with home managers to handle disagreements over release, priorities etc. We suggest that these SLAs also set out clearly the process for handling such performance issues as:

☐ Who is responsible for coaching and counselling in the first instance?

☐ Is the process totally informal and unrecorded, or will it have some formality and be recorded?

☐ Who else might be involved in such sessions, eg home manager, HR professional?

☐ If the process is recorded, who receives the information, and for what purpose?

☐ How does the process fit in with the organisation's disciplinary process?

2 This might seem a rather onerous and unnecessary exercise. However, performance issues are often not addressed because people are not clear about responsibilities and the process. Also, standard SLAs can be drawn up that can then be used, with perhaps a little modification, in all cases.

3 Consider including among the task objectives for all project team members some that relate to interpersonal and team behaviours (akin to Roberts' KPAs mentioned earlier). This establishes that these behaviours are important and will be monitored.

---

4 In Chapter 3 we set up the concept of team feedback contracts. Consider setting up some form of regular processes on these behaviours (eg questionnaires) for getting feedback from team members on each other. This could be extended to full team feedback to include everyone who deals with each team member on a regular basis, eg support team members, client or sponsor. Remember that the feedback can and should be positive as well as negative: it is important that superior performance and behaviour are recognised.

We have covered so far the day-to-day management of individuals' performance to ensure that the project objectives are achieved and that variances in performance are addressed. We move on next to another key aspect of performance management: the training and development of project team members.

Training and development of project team members

A critical area of difference we identified at the outset between stable team and project team working is the issue of several bosses. In the previous section we looked at this in the context of the everyday handling of performance management. Here we look at who is responsible for the training and development and, in particular, the long-term development, of team members.

Training for the project

First we look at the issues concerning the training needs for the project itself. From Chapter 2 it would appear that the training needs for project team members at the outset of the project are fairly limited, as usually only staff with the appropriate expertise are recruited to projects. Occasionally, there will be a need for the acquisition of specific knowledge or skill; for example, Robinson of Eastern Group mentioned learning about the generating industry. However, there can be important training needs associated with the effective running of the project, for example:

☐ learning to use the appropriate software package for the planning, monitoring, and control of projects. (In the LT

Strategic HR Unit all the staff were trained to use Microsoft Project.)

☐ training and development arising out of the need to establish sound team processes (see Chapter 3) – for example, problem-solving skills or conflict-handling skills. (In Eastern Group, Roberts' project team was trained in the particular BPR approach that was going to be used on the project.)

☐ training and development to cover any gaps in the key personal skills required by project team members (see Chapter 2).

☐ training for key roles such as the project leader and the project manager/administrator (see Chapter 2). The project leader may be a professional project leader, as is the case in ICL, but elsewhere he or she is often appointed on the basis of a particular expertise. For example, Robinson in Eastern Group remarked that he felt he would have benefited from training in project leader skills. Some organisations (Leveson, 1996) do encourage their professionals to supplement their core expertise with project leadership/ management skills.

Responsibility for training and development

In stable teams there is little problem about who is responsible for training and development: it traditionally falls to the functional line manager. Our experience and research have shown that, not unexpectedly, the identification of project-related training needs for team members during the project is usually the responsibility of the project leader. The problems arise with long-term development needs for those involved in project and matrix working for a significant part of their time. It is asking quite a lot of the task-focused project leaders to expect them to take time out to consider something that will only come to fruition *after* the project is completed and when they no longer have any responsibility for their former charges. Similarly, there is the danger that the home or functional manager may lose a certain interest in the long-term development of a member of staff who, for the foreseeable future, might be assigned to someone else's workforce and if, as was

Roberts' experience on the Eastern Group BPR project, the members of successful project teams move on afterwards to greater things.

So who does look after the formal appraisal and development needs of project team members? We came across some interesting models:

☐ In the LT Strategic HR Unit a system operates whereby everyone has a personal coach who will carry out, among other things, the regular quarterly and end-of-year managing personal development (MPD) interviews as well as the Unit's twice-monthly *folder* meetings. The coach is often the person's team leader, but this is not necessarily always the case – for example, Vessey's coach is one of his colleagues. Where a person works on more than one project in the Unit (as is usually the case) the individual consolidates the competing objectives for discussion with their coach. The project leader agrees the individual's project-related objectives and reviews these against performance on the projects, each project leader supplying formal reports to the coach on the extent to which the objectives have been achieved.

☐ Under Eastern Group's performance management scheme there are six-monthly reviews. In the BPR project Roberts, as project leader, took on the full responsibility. He set up additional monthly reviews and saw these as a 'major part of my role of managing the team'. So far as development of an individual was concerned, the opportunity of working on a big project, such as the one led by Roberts, was seen as developmental in itself. To quote Roberts:

> Peoples' long-term development needs were addressed by working on the project. This raised their profiles, made them more saleable; every single person went back to a better job.

☐ In ICL some of the review and appraisal responsibilities are covered in the project leader's job description:

> *Staff:* Implement processes to ensure the regular review (and appraisal where appropriate) of the performance of all staff resources allocated to the project.
>
> (ICL, 1995)

However, the role will be shared with the home manager, depending on the extent of the involvement in and the length of the project. The project leader 'operates in a matrix role with the line management functions within the business' in all their people management roles. May of ICL describes their performance management scheme in these terms:

> Most people will have a home manager who will...look across all the projects and deal with future development. Project leaders will set task objectives for the project, the home manager will set personal (developmental) objectives. If there is a conflict the home manager will sort it out.

☐ A major consultancy operating internationally in the information services arena and specialising in the handling of change associated with BPR is organised on a project team basis. The consultancy uses a system of mentors to manage their performance development system, which has an annual cycle. The goals, which must include at least one personal development goal (and, interestingly, a goal related to company growth), are agreed at the outset. There is a formal assessment at the six-month and twelve-month stages against those goals. The mentor is responsible for collecting performance information from everyone who has dealt with the individual – for example, all project leaders, clients, etc (it is intended to be based on a full 360° feedback process). The mentor conducts the review session and grades the individual. At the twelve-month stage this grading is used by the team leader of the individual for determining pay. Mentors are drawn from within the organisation.

☐ A very similar approach was described by Howell and Cameron (1996) regarding the introduction of mentors at the software systems company Science Systems. The major difference from the previous example was that the mentors were outside consultants.

It is clear to us that there are potential pitfalls in ensuring that the long-term development needs of project team members are met. There is always the danger that someone who is *good at* project working and regularly invited to join project teams could find that the task objectives were always getting in the way of long-term development. May of ICL commented that this gap was recognised within the company, in that:

> there is still a role for the home manager with regard to long-term employability or to meet Company strategic objectives. However, there is not always a separate home manager for long-term development of those people on large projects which extend over many months, even years.

In addition there can be the issue of the individual's long-term development needs which are not perceived to be relevant to the home manager's middle- to long-term needs, and certainly will be far removed from the project leader's agenda. This is not considered to be an issue in some organisations – for example, in Rank Xerox, where Bater told us the culture was one in which 'people are trained for career development, not just for a job'. They find this encourages multiskilling, horizontal moves, and flexibility, thus promoting mobility across and upward in the company and *outside*! However, in many organisations where project working is becoming an increasingly important activity, this gap needs to be addressed.

Self-managing your personal and professional development

There has been increasing emphasis on individuals' taking responsibility for their own development as part of the move to the Holy Grail of the learning organisation. *We suggest that this may be an essential requirement for individuals working in a project environment.* The characteristic of independence needed by project team members discussed in Chapter 2 should extend beyond the way they handle their project work to the way they handle their own development. In the dynamic and complex world of project working, long-term personal and professional development is too important to leave to others. In the world of fast-track careers there can be a narrow window of opportunity where a particular experience or training intervention is appropriate and supports that career progress. We believe that only the individual concerned has the detailed knowledge of all the issues involved to be able to determine the balance between short-term project needs and the long-term needs of a personal and professional nature. That is not to say that the organisation should not support and help the individual, for example through the use of coaches and mentors as described earlier, but that the primary responsibility has to be with the individual.

ICL has started to go down the route of encouraging people to take more responsibility for their own learning. They have not yet formally assessed how this is working, but already recognise that it is in fact a major culture change and that there needs to be substantial reinforcement in the workplace. This view is supported by the experience of a training and development professional in one of the large consultancy practices, who found that the reluctance of professionals to take control of their own training extended to their managers' own development as well (Croft, 1996). One organisation that has recognised that introducing 'employee self-development' required a substantial change process was the software company Santa Cruz Operation (Macaulay and Harding, 1996).

In the University of Westminster there is a tradition of self-identification of both short- and long-term development needs. It is only in relatively recent times that any formal performance development system has been used. It is perhaps not surprising in an 'educational' industry that the culture of self-development is well established. It is also interesting to surmise the extent to which it is also related to the very independent style of working that operates in most universities.

The Strategic HR Unit in LT has also gone a considerable way along this road. Under their MPD system the individual has the proactive role, but in partnership with the project leader and coach. For example:

☐ The individual is responsible for 'identifying training and development needs (both personal and project-related) with project leaders/coaches and incorporating these into the learning contract'.

☐ The project leader 'provides the individual with coaching support for both personal and project-related development needs'.

☐ The MPD coach 'discusses development needs (both

personal and project-related) and ensures they are acted upon'.   (LUL 1996)

We believe that the people challenge of ensuring that project team members, including project leaders, do not miss out on long-term development is two-fold:

☐ encouraging a culture in which the individual takes responsibility for his or her own development

☐ providing the appropriate support by the organisation to maximise the potential of all their people.

Strategies for the training and development of project team members

1 Ensure that people in the key roles, eg project leader/manager, are appropriately trained in the project management processes and other key skills identified in Chapter 2. If the project leader/manager is not a professional in project working (unlike in ICL), consider providing him or her with focused training immediately prior to taking up his or her project role.

2 Ensure that project team members are equipped with the appropriate skills for project teamworking (see Chapter 2).

3 Give the project leader clear responsibility for the training associated with the project – if necessary provide development/support in how to identify and meet these training needs.

4 Consider setting up a system of coaches or mentors whose primary responsibility is to support individuals in their longer-term development. This role can be taken on by individuals' home manager, but it must be made clear that they themselves have this specific responsibility.

5 Introduce a system that helps individuals to keep track of their own competencies. For example, one organisation has set up a computer system which can be accessed by all their people and which lists the core competencies, plus the facility to add more. The staff are encouraged to grade themselves against these competencies, with the opportunity to list those in which they have no current knowledge or skill but would like to

develop.

6 Set up career management workshops which focus on:

☐ developing learning skills

☐ how to access development opportunities

☐ assessing competencies

☐ preparing and implementing learning plans.

Do not see these as one-off interventions – best of all, encourage everyone to attend regular workshops throughout the year.

7 Encourage a project environment where learning is part of the job (see Chapter 5 for strategies to help here).

The importance of this attention to people's wider training and development needs was beautifully summed up by Whitfield of ICL in relation to the motivation of project team members: 'Do your best by others' careers and they will do their best by you.'

Motivating the individual and the team

We have described the aim of becoming a learning organisation as the current Holy Grail. Perhaps the most persistent search since that for the Holy Grail has been in the area of motivation. The one certainty that has come out of the vast quantity of research and theories that abound in this field is that motivation is a very complex subject. We have touched on it in the previous sections – not surprisingly, as motivation is affected in some way by almost every aspect of working life. It is not our intention here to look at motivation generally, but to highlight what we believe to be the special differences between project team and stable team working in the challenge of motivating the individual and the team.

Project team working *can*, if properly organised and managed, provide a number of definite plus points:

☐ the clarity of overall project and individuals' objectives. Locke's goal-setting theory (Locke, 1968) proposes that motivation is increased when individuals are set specific performance goals. Locke emphasises that the goals should be seen as fair and reasonable by the employees, and the latter should participate in the goal-setting process for it to be motivational. This strongly supports our view that project team members should be given ownership of the objective-setting process.

☐ regular and focused feedback on performance. Locke's theory also emphasises the importance of feedback on the attainment of individuals' goals. This is inherent in the strong monitoring and control systems usually in place in projects.

☐ the breaking down of the project into tasks in such a way that individuals can see how their part contributes to the whole (using the WBS process and Gantt charts).

☐ strong mutual interdependency. Whitfield of ICL, talking about motivation, offered the view that 'It all comes back to shared purpose and interdependency' that exists between project team members.

☐ the often challenging and developmental nature of the work. May of ICL talked about motivators as generally intrinsic to project work, and about project working providing:

> ☐ interesting issues for people to work on
>
> ☐ technically challenging work.

Challenging work and opportunity to grow in your job were two of Herzberg's motivational factors (Herzberg, 1966) and form part of the *self-actualisation* pinnacle of Maslow's hierarchy of needs (Maslow, 1970). Herzberg's work helped to focus attention on the concepts of job enrichment and job rotation. Project working can provide excellent examples of both.

☐ the opportunity for greater responsibility offered by the often looser style of supervision in project teams. This is another of Herzberg's motivators.

☐ the enhancing of an individual's career – particularly if the project is prestigious and high-profile. Roberts of Eastern

Group talked about making people more 'saleable' and 'raising their profile': 'Every single person went back to a better job.' Advancement is another of Herzberg's motivators, and realisation of potential forms part of the highest level of Maslow's hierarchy of needs.

The potential motivational problem areas with project working can be:

☐ conflicts in objectives caused by multiproject working which, if not addressed, negate Locke's theories.

☐ the reality that the 'social needs' for relationships, affection, and a sense of belonging (from Maslow's hierarchy of needs) can be less well served by project working than by working as part of a stable team

☐ poor supervision – the looser supervision that characterises much project working can be either a motivator or de-motivator. If that looser supervision also incorporates a lack of support and constructive feedback then it can turn into one of Herzberg's hygiene factors which cause dissatisfaction.

☐ pressure – another double-edged sword of project working. The right amount can be stimulating, too much can be debilitating. Pressure goes hand-in-hand with project working because of the usually tight time-scales and the frequent need to juggle with competing demands from different projects.

☐ security – project working is by its nature transient. This is another of Herzberg's factors that can lead to dissatisfaction. It is also one of the basic needs in Maslow's hierarchy. In Chapter 5 we look at ways of dealing with this issue.

We have discussed so far the issues that affect *individual* motivation. That of team motivation is much less commonly addressed. In part it is the sum of individuals' motivation, but it is also that spiralling of enthusiasm and energy that comes from working as part of a motivated team. Perhaps its strongest evocation is found in Senge's concept of aligned objectives and shared vision (Senge, 1990). (See Chapter 2.) Motivation is often seen as the role of the leader; in this case it would be the project leader. We argue that it is a role that can and should be shared with the whole team. This is particularly important given the strong task-focus of the project leader. Every individual team member can adversely affect the motivation of the team – by having non-aligned objectives, operating without regard to team relationships, or failing to perform. People are often remarkably unaware of the demotivating effects of their behaviour on others. Happily, the reverse can also apply: enthusiasm and commitment can be mutually stimulating.

Most of the strategies for addressing the people challenges of motivating the individual and the team have been covered earlier – for example, the setting of clear objectives, giving feedback, developing strong team relationships – or will be covered in some detail in the following chapter – for example, dealing with insecurity.

The additional strategies for motivating the individual and the team

1 Make people feel valued. Roberts of Eastern Group made a point of making team members feel important and valued by emphasising their special selection for the project and 'making time to discuss their jobs with them'.

2 Give the project team responsibility for motivation:

☐ Raise awareness of the impact of individuals' behaviour on others and on team motivation by specifically covering the issue in the team integration workshop in Chapter 3.

☐ Put motivation on the agenda of project team meetings!

3 Consider using motivation surveys at regular points in the project's life cycle to monitor how the project team, and perhaps also the support team, are feeling about their work.

We look next at the area of extrinsic reward – through pay, bonuses, perks etc.

Rewarding the individual and the team
The concepts of performance management, motivation, and reward are usually discussed together because of the obvious

links between them. The degree to which financial rewards are a motivator is a complex subject and undoubtedly varies between individuals and for an individual over time. There has been considerable focus on individual performance-related pay (PRP) in recent years, but problem issues have remained, such as:

☐ the difficulty of deciding the bases on which the performance–pay link should be established
☐ the problems of using the performance appraisal systems both for decisions on pay and as a basis for making staff development decisions
☐ the extent to which individual PRP is worthwhile in money terms.

The suggestion is that these types of scheme are on the decline and the emphasis is turning towards team pay:

> The focus is now shifting away from individual performance-related pay (PRP), which has failed conspicuously to deliver results in many instances, and turning towards team pay and other methods of rewarding the whole team.
>
> (Armstrong, 1996)

Many argue that individual PRP actually *hampers* team performance because:

☐ it encourages (not surprisingly) individual team members to concentrate on their own objectives, which can be at the expense of those of the team
☐ it does not encourage the concept of working as a team towards the team goals
☐ it may lead managers to concentrate on individual rather than team performance.

Peters (1987) unequivocally states under his list of successful factors for team development that: 'Rewards should go to the team as a whole'! We have been involved with PRP systems in the past and are as committed as Peters to the concept of team, rather than individual, rewards for project teamworking.

Table 6

RESEARCH INTO TEAM PAY

Research results – team pay works best for teams that:	Project teams:
☐ 'stand alone as performing units for which clear targets and standards can be agreed	☐ are by definition stand-alone performance units set up for specific purposes and usually with very clear targets
☐ have a considerable degree of autonomy...teams, that are, to a large degree, self-managed	☐ are often managed by project leaders who lead through a facilitation and support role – we advocate team empowerment
☐ are composed of people whose work is interdependent and where it is acknowledged by members that the team will deliver only if they work well together and share responsibility for success	☐ are by definition composed of people whose work is interdependent
☐ are stable, where members are used to working with one another, know what is expected of them by fellow team members and know where they stand in the regard of their colleagues	☐ are not stable teams, but if the effort is made to establish team processes (as set out in Chapter 3) then the project team should have many of these features
☐ are mature, where teams are well established, used to working flexibly to meet targets, and are capable of making good use of the complementary skills of their members	☐ have to work hard to gain maturity (see Chapter 3), but flexibility and the ability to make use of others' complementary skills are key characteristics of project team members
☐ are composed of individuals who are flexible, multi-skilled, and good team players while still being capable of expressing a different point of view and carrying that point if it is for the good of the team.' (Armstrong, 1996)	☐ if selected according to the criteria set out in Chapter 2 will be made up of members with these characteristics

Armstrong (1996) summarises the results of an IPD research project into pay, which suggested that team pay works best for teams with many of the characteristics of project teams. We set out in Table 6 the special characteristics of project teamworking alongside Armstrong's results.

If team pay is being considered there still remain three important and potentially problematical issues:

☐ How much should team bonus payments be in terms of the proportion of the overall remuneration of individuals? There is the same debate as for individual PRP on making it a sufficiently high proportion to be an incentive but not too high to cause insecurity in terms of financial planning.

☐ How should the team payment be assessed – on what criteria? For example, it could be linked to meeting or beating milestones, cost targets etc.

☐ How should team pay be allocated to team members? Who should be eligible? Should it be all team members or only some – do you include part-time as well as full-time members? What about the 'invisible' team (the support team) – surely their support should be recognised and rewarded in some way? Should you give everyone the same payment, ie simply divide the team payment by the number of eligible team members, or should you relate it in some way to salary (say, as a percentage) or perhaps to the time people were involved (some sort of input measure)? Or should pay be related to performance (some sort of output measure), and if so, how? If it is related to performance you are back to the problems of individual PRP schemes!

Our experience and research suggest that not many organisations have progressed very far on team pay. This view was supported by Armstrong (1996), who quoted a survey that showed only 14 per cent of organisations 'expected to introduce team-based rewards below senior management level in the next two years'. There was quite a range of answers from those contributing to our research to the question of how they dealt with rewards to project team members:

☐ In the LT Strategic HR Unit there is no special reward scheme for project workers. All managers are on a company-wide, individual, performance-related pay system. Team leaders set the performance element of pay for their teams and this can vary from nothing for below-standard performance, through a company-standard increase, to a bigger increase for those rated as excellent performers throughout the year. Team leaders gather performance data from the project leaders, taking into account all the projects that an individual has worked on over the year, to arrive at their decision.

☐ The University of Westminster has had a scheme of performance-related pay in which all academic staff can nominate any other member of staff to receive a performance award. This nomination has not just been related to their work on project teams but applies also to their *normal* work.

☐ In Rank Xerox there is a system of reward and recognition for project teams that is based on the dual standards of:

☐ how well the project team followed the process (or went round the company 'quality wheel')

☐ what level of performance the team achieved against project objectives – for example, in terms of quality, cost, and cycle time improvement.

There can be a team bonus which ranges between £200 and £1,500 per team member based on their contribution, ie a combination of team and individual performance. The level of contribution is judged by the appropriate process area manager, who is not necessarily the line manager of the project team member. Recognition can also be in the form of a dinner or small gift.

☐ In ICL they also have a performance-related pay scheme, but the emphasis is on personal rather than team objectives.

☐ Eastern Group has an individual PRP system which, in theory, can pay up to 20 per cent of salary. In reality the amount is usually rather less. Project team members can receive a cash bonus for a job well done, be taken out for a social event, or receive a nice letter from a director! Where an Eastern Group project team has been successful it is generally assumed that each team member made an equal contribution to that success and the payment will be calculated accordingly.

There are no easy or prescriptive answers on reward schemes.

They depend on a whole range of factors, not least the culture of the organisation. It is interesting to note the experience of some universities who introduced individual PRP for the lecturing staff in the form of bonuses. The move was opposed by many on the lecturing staff who, faced with no choice, effectively tailored the system to suit themselves. One team decided who would be nominated for the bonuses, and then that individual divided the bonus equally between the team members, ie they opted for a team-pay approach! The message from this is that it might well be worth consulting the project team about how they would want any team performance-related bonuses distributed – there is no point in having a system that is considered either unfair or inappropriate, as (fairly obviously) it is likely to have the opposite effect to that intended!

Strategies for financial rewards

1 If performance-related pay schemes are planned, consider introducing *team* pay schemes. Project teams are by their nature particularly suited to this type of approach.

2 Consider empowering the team to decide how any team bonus should be distributed. This would best be approached early in the project but *after* the team has completed 'the getting the team working stage', when the team might be best placed to discuss this sensitive issue:

☐ Table the issue for a project team meeting.

☐ Formally introduce the issues and set out the options so that people are aware of the opportunities and any limitations.

☐ Encourage creative ideas – for example, using the team bonus for a trip or event. (One team we are aware of chose to donate the money to a charity of their choice.)

However, remember that the non-financial rewards discussed in the last section (for example, positive feedback and challenging and interesting work) can be powerful motivators.

Many, including ourselves, would argue that for the knowledge workers of the future these are the more effective motivators.

Conclusion

Delivering results in project teams depends on the individual team members and the team as a whole working at optimum performance – perhaps one of the most complex as well as key people challenges of managing in the project environment. The foundations for success will have been set in the team integration and development phase described in the previous chapter. It is then a matter of having appropriate systems and processes in place (for example, for the setting of clear objectives and their monitoring and control, for handling variances in performance, and for addressing the crucial issue of team members' long-term development needs). Finally it is a matter of how to motivate and reward the team so as to ensure that the team is committed to operating at peak performance throughout the project life cycle.

5

MOVING ONWARDS

Introduction

We have now reached the phase in the project's life when the major work has been completed and the end is clearly in sight – the phase that we and other writers call rather starkly 'run-down/termination'. The very terminology suggests that it is the twilight period of the project and, by implication, of the project team. Some writers express it even more bleakly, calling the phase 'declining' and 'death'.

The same rather sad and downbeat feeling is reflected in the title of the last stage of the team development cycle – the 'mourning' stage. That is why we have called our stage of the project team cycle the more positive 'Moving Onwards'. All projects will reach an end either (hopefully) when they are successfully completed or sometimes prematurely if the need for, or priority of, the project changes. Project working almost by definition means moving on. As the traditional terminology suggests, it is a stage that people can find difficult, worrying, and sad, one that leaves them with a sense of loss. It will often come after a period of peak performance, the project team working very hard and at optimum effectiveness – the stage when morale is usually at its highest. After all, the team is delivering the results, and doing so perhaps after quite a long period of planning and preparation. Therefore it is not surprising that this final stage can come as quite a shock to the system – or rather as an anti-climax after all the activity of the previous stages. A major challenge is to look on this final stage as a positive one – one of moving on and forwards.

One of the key differences between working in stable teams and project teams is the sure and certain fact that, however large and complex the project is, it will at some stage come to an end and the team be disbanded. However, although this is a fairly obvious feature, it is one in which the people challenges are perhaps overlooked. We see the specific people challenges of this phase as these:

☐ The project will start to lose its resources. This may be in a planned way matching the decline in needs of the project. However, sometimes it will be in an unplanned way as 'other projects will start receiving a greater share of the resources and attention. Some may steal resources ...' (Geddes *et al*, 1990). On the other hand, as team members see the end of the project approaching they may choose to leave earlier than expected if the appropriate opportunity comes along. Therefore there may be a problem of insufficient resources in the final stage.

☐ The team will start to break up. There may have been changes along the way but this time the changes will be major and mostly all one way – out of the project. There can be important issues about maintaining the morale and motivation of those who are left – the *survivors*.

☐ Planning the move of team members on to other work. This may be back into their home functional or departmental teams (where there may be *re-entry* problems), into other projects, or out of the organisation all together. Doing right by people becomes an important maxim: to quote Whitfield of ICL again 'Do your best by others' careers and they will do their best by you.' It is important that these moves out of the project are planned to maximise the interests of the individuals concerned and, equally important, that they are seen to do so.

☐ Maximising the learning from the project for individuals, the team, and the organisation. There will undoubtedly have been valuable learning experiences on the project – from the successes *and* the failures – and it is important that these are captured and analysed for future use.

☐ Celebrating the end of the project. This is a matter of celebrating what the project has achieved for the individual, the team, and the organisation. It might be considered quite normal and relatively easy to do if the project has been successful, ie achieved its objectives. However, sometimes projects achieve their objectives with a lot of pain. On the other hand, those projects that are less successful or fall by the wayside will still have some achievements to celebrate.

This is a stage of the project that receives very little attention in the literature or indeed is rarely seen as an issue in its own right by our practitioners. Probably this is because, as we have discussed earlier, project management is very focused on the task, and the energies of all involved are directed to achieving the final milestone. As organisations move towards matrix management and greater use of project working, the issue of how projects end and how the team is disbanded is likely to take a higher profile because of the impact on the people involved. We now look in detail at each of the people challenges outlined above.

Matching people resources to workload during the project rundown

In an ideal world the project plan would show the phased rundown of the resources required for the final stages, and there would be an orderly exit of the right people at the right time. In the real world, however, a number of factors can intervene to affect the precision of this planning:

☐ The project may overrun and team members may have to leave before their part of the work is completed. With good planning and control systems this should be foreseen, and there should be the opportunity to make alternative arrangements. Perhaps the team members affected might work part-time on the project, or another team member be given the responsibility for the work that is left.

☐ The estimate of resources required in the rundown phase may have been wrong. These can be very tricky to estimate. Unforeseen problems may occur. For example, in the handover of a new computer system, teething problems could occur in the initial use of the system; in a major change project it might be decided that further interventions are required to bed the changes down etc. By their nature these problems are difficult to anticipate – in an environment of tight resources it is hard to plan the allocation of resources for such contingencies (for example, by building in slack).

☐ Other more urgent or higher-priority projects may come along and 'steal' some of the resources. This may result in the project being delayed by agreement or, more usually, in the remaining team just being expected to cope.

☐ Opportunities of other work may emerge for team members and the team or organisation may choose to release them early.

Being underresourced at this stage may not seem too important – after all, the project is all but completed. However, the way the 'loose ends' are dealt with can leave that final vital impression of the project with the client or customer. Handling it badly by prolonging the last stages through under-resourcing may dissipate all the goodwill that has so far been built up with the project. In fact this is surprisingly common. Anyone who has ever been involved with a construction project will recognise this issue. It is the snagging stage that can destroy a previously good relationship with a builder, when there appears to be no interest or momentum to sort out these annoying, small problems. The builder's team has moved on to its next piece of work, and it is clear that one's own project is now a very low priority. IT projects are an equally good example, where it is in the early stages of implementation of the new system that the project's reputation can be made or broken.

Another good example involved a project set up to reorganise and restructure an organisation. The new structure was brought in, staff were appointed to it, and a major programme of internal customer care training was carried out involving all the staff. The project was perceived as being completed and resources for it were largely withdrawn. It was acknowledged that there were some important but 'tidying-up' activities still to be completed – preparing detailed roles and responsibilities and ensuring these were shared with everyone was one such. However, because the dedicated project resources were almost gone, these last tasks took a long time. During this period the staff lost their initial enthusiasm and commitment to the reorganisation and change process.

Equally destructive is the effect that this can have on the remaining project team, who see themselves struggling to complete those final activities and perhaps receiving little support or recognition from the major stakeholders or the organisation at large. It is likely that for that part of the team, the project will end on a sour note.

Strategies for matching the people resources to workload during the project rundown

1 Ensure that the planning for the final stage of the project is as well researched as for the earlier, sometime perceived as more challenging, stages.

2 Identify clearly what the 'wrap-up work' (Frame, 1995) involves. Ensure that these activities are given the same status as activities in the mainstream of the project.

3 Make sure that communication channels are maintained with the major stakeholders – the client/customer/sponsor – throughout this stage. Although the momentum of the project is clearly slowing down, it is important that the *managing* team does not lose sight of the project.

4 Maintain excellent relationships with the major controllers of resources in the organisation – usually the functional or departmental heads – because you may need their support at this stage.

5 Let the project team take ownership of the problem – they may be able to solve it through more imaginative use of the team's resources or through their informal networks back in their own departments.

Less commonly these days, the mismatch can be the other way round, with the project left with a surplus of resources. This can cause rather different problems. It can exacerbate any feeling of insecurity if team members feel that there is no work for them on the project or, at that time, elsewhere in the organisation.

> **Strategies for dealing with this situation**
>
> 1 Encourage the team members involved to use spare time in a structured way – considering their next career move, preparing CVs if relevant, or training in 'job move' or any other relevant skills.
>
> 2 Consider whether there are any learning opportunities for them in teaming up with other active team members on the remaining tasks of the project in order to learn their skills.
>
> 3 Consider using them as a task team to evaluate how the project has gone – see later in this chapter.

Maintaining the morale and motivation of the remaining team

This can be a very sensitive time for the project team. It will just have completed the intense activity phase of delivering results, when team spirit and morale are likely to have been at their highest. The project team is now faced with a loss of members, combined with a change in the pace and often in the nature of the work. Hardingham and Royal (1994) warn that 'commitment may surge or dip depending on how disbanding the team is handled'. Quite a considerable amount of literature has recently been devoted to the (in some ways) rather analogous situation of *survivors* – the people who remain in their jobs – after the downsizing exercises of the last few years. The literature shows that as a result of a number of factors – the often stressful lead into and process of downsizing itself, and the pressure of tight resourcing following the cutbacks – the survivors were themselves highly stressed. However, a major factor was also found to be the loss of friends and colleagues from their own teams and the break-up of support networks built up over many years. In the same way, on a project team – particularly those which have existed over a long period of time and in which a strong bonding and sense of teamworking has built up – the loss of that team framework can be a shock, a source of sadness, and a cause of stress.

This may be combined with the remaining team working on what might appear to be low-prestige work: the tying-up of the loose ends. It might also be rather unrewarding work, dealing with minor problems in an atmosphere of customer irritability. It may also be seen to lack challenge, with no new learning or development to be gained from it. Furthermore, there will be a temptation to be looking ahead to the next project or the return to the home department. These factors, combined with the loss of valued colleagues and the team framework, may easily cause a loss of motivation or morale. The challenge is to keep the remaining team focused on the project and motivated.

Strategies for maintaining morale and motivation

1 Increase the frequency of project team meetings. Often the reverse happens, as there is a decreasing amount of business to be discussed. However, the meetings can play a vital part in keeping the remaining team operating in a cohesive and committed way.

2 Take time to explore with the team how the changes have affected the way the team works. For example, revisit the Belbin profiles and look at how the balance of informal team roles has changed. Encourage the team to fill the gaps by operating on their subsidiary strengths, or get their agreement that perhaps some roles are less crucial at this stage (for example, the Plant – the ideas person). The key roles to fill during this phase will be the:

☐ Completer/Finisher (for fairly obvious reasons!)

☐ Chairman/Co-ordinator to hold the team together and keep it focused

☐ Monitor/Evaluator – this can be a problem-solving period

☐ Team Worker – that useful role which lends a sympathetic ear to other team members' worries and concerns.

3 Encourage team members to keep in contact with others who

have left, emphasising the value of having wide support networks of colleagues.

4 Emphasise the importance of the work at this stage. Spell out the relevance, for example, of providing good documentation for the new product or system. Enlist the help of the major stake-holders – customer/client/sponsor – to support this.

5 Use the team to start the evaluation and review process – it can provide the challenge and developmental learning from this stage of the project (see later).

Planning the moves on to other work

Keeping the team together, focused on and committed to the project at this stage will depend critically on how individual team members view the future beyond the project. If we return to the concept of aligning objectives, the individual's objectives at this stage are likely to centre on identifying the appropriate next move. For some team members, those that are full time on the project, this will be a major issue. For others, working part time on the project, it may be of much less significance. For short projects it may well not be an issue at all. In some cases there will be complete certainty: perhaps the individual had been seconded to the project from his or her own depart-ment and will return to it on completion of the project. However, individuals may still be concerned about what type of work they will return to, whom they will be working for and with etc. For others, there may be the certainty of work else-where in the organisation but uncertainty again about the nature of the work, colleagues etc. At the far end of the spec-trum are those team members who have perhaps been brought in on short-term contracts for the particular project. Their future may be solely in their own hands, ie it may lie in finding further contract work. Most project team members are likely to feel some anxiety about the future.

The people challenge is to acknowledge that anxiety and work to resolve it as far as possible.

Strategies for planning the moves on to other work

1 Prepare an exit plan for team members. Consider calling it something amusing, for example, 'The Great Escape Plan' or, if you want to inject a more positive note, 'The Mighty Moving Plan'. At an appropriate time (about four months) before the expected beginning of the rundown of the people resources in the project, discuss at a project team meeting how the plan will work:

☐ It will identify the likely date on which each team member is to leave the project.

☐ About three months before that date, the project leader, home manager, or the relevant member of the HR department (or any combination of these) will sit down with each team member and discuss his or her needs and aspirations for the next move. At that point a suitable mentor to help the individual through the moving process will be identified, which could be any of those listed earlier, the coach or mentor identified in Chapter 4, or someone chosen specifically for this role.

☐ Each team member will be encouraged to draw up a personal moving plan (PMP), which sets out the activities to be undertaken by that individual and any others involved, with time-scales. The PMP could include activities like preparing a CV, discussing the CV with an appropriate mentor, training or coaching in interview skills, setting up meetings with prospective employers, or undertaking training to improve employability.

☐ The team member will be encouraged to be proactive in setting up regular review meetings with his or her mentor to monitor progress through the plan.

2 Encourage the team to see the moving-on process as part of the overall project. At the appropriate time The Mighty Moving Plan would become a regular agenda item for project team meetings. This has the double advantage of making the process appear part of the normal life of the project, rather than something special or unusual, and also of enabling the team to support individual team members in this activity just as in others. Team members can feel very alone at this time – after

> all, who is interested in or cares about their career except them-
> selves? Although it is clearly important that each individual
> takes responsibility for his or her own career, actively harness-
> ing the team's support can be a very positive influence. It can
> also be useful in rebuilding team motivation.

Even for those team members whose future seems reasonably
assured, the processes described above can be very beneficial.
Any exposure to change can cause anxiety, so the simple
processes of making it visible, planning for it, and taking
control of what seems (and often is) an uncertain situation will
help reduce anxiety.

Maximising the learning from the project

It will be a rare project where there have not been valuable
learning experiences for the individuals, team, and organisation. In fact, for many it is the opportunity for a learning
experience that attracts them to a particular project in the first
place. As we outlined in Chapter 3, this is a powerful way of
aligning personal goals with those of the project.

Individual and team learning

What do we mean by 'learning'? Swieringa and Wierdsma
(1992) make the powerful point that learning is about changing behaviour. They define it as follows:

> The goal of this change in behaviour is to arrive at a form of
> behaviour which corresponds better to the goals of the learner;
> in other words, behaviour that is more effective. We call this
> competence.

They argue that learning is often equated with the increasing
of knowledge, but that the key to the development of competence is much wider:

> Competence is not determined only by what people know or
> understand but also by what they can do (skills), what they have
> the *courage* and *will* to do and who they *are* (personality and
> attitude).

Projects can provide a very fertile source of learning:

- Clearly there can be knowledge-learning in terms within particular subject areas. Robinson at Eastern Group talked about the need to learn about generating plants, Roberts about benchmarking; Vessey at LT referred to knowledge gained from having to research into such areas as reward systems.

- There can be knowledge- and skills-learning specifically to do with managing and being involved in project working. For example, in the LT Strategic HR Unit everyone was trained to use the software package (Microsoft Project) for planning and monitoring projects. It will be rare for most project team members to escape without an improved understanding of planning and monitoring budgets!

- There can be the often surprising and fascinating learning from working closely with people from other functions. For people in support functions, it can provide insights into the operational side of the business that it would be hard to replicate without actually working there. For example, in a project set up to design a large training programme for supervisory staff, personnel and training people worked closely with operational supervisors and their managers on the team. Working on the project to build a house at the Ideal Home Exhibition, we learned a lot about what was involved in the marketing aspects of such an event.

- There can be the learning associated with coming into contact with the most senior members of an organisation – how to work with senior people, how they themselves operate in (for example) steering group sessions, what issues concern them etc.

- Last but by no means least, there can be the learning associated from working on a team with the need to deliver a specified product against a tight timetable. There will be the learning of how teams work in these situations, how project leaders and other team members handle conflict and pressure, and how you yourself use your interpersonal skills to handle challenging situations.

Much of this learning comes from actually working on the project rather than through more formal training and development interventions. In terms of the Kolb learning cycle (see Figure 6) it is through the process of experiencing an event and then reflecting on what has happened, analysing and generating theories about the experience, deciding on a different course of action or behaviour, and then putting that into practice. This is referred to as 'experiential learning', 'learning by doing'; Kolb (1974) himself preferred to speak of 'problem-oriented learning'.

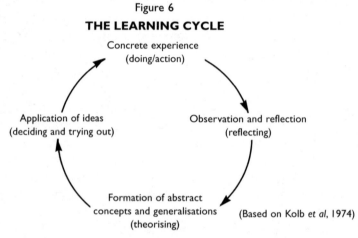

Figure 6

THE LEARNING CYCLE

Concrete experience
(doing/action)

Application of ideas
(deciding and trying out)

Observation and reflection
(reflecting)

Formation of abstract
concepts and generalisations
(theorising)

(Based on Kolb et al, 1974)

For learning to take place in this way it requires the individual to go round the cycle. Associated with Kolb's theory is the contention that people have a natural preference for learning in a particular way. Honey and Mumford (1992) conclude that there are four main learning styles – activists, reflectors, theorists, and pragmatists – associated with the different stages in the cycle. Thomas summarises these as follows:

...for the *activist*, new experiences, challenges and problems, with opportunities to generate ideas will stimulate the learning process...

The *reflector* will learn best where time is given to preparation and thinking, time to watch and listen and mull over things...

The *theorist* will learn best from activities where a clear purpose is given together with time to explore the system and process...They will not learn well from demonstrations without being given the theoretical basis as well...

The *pragmatist* learns best from activities where techniques are shown by someone who has expertise in the subject...There will be a wish to try things out and practise with lots of examples... (Thomas 1995)

It could be argued that the type of experiential learning encountered on projects is best suited to activists. The people challenge is to enhance all team members' abilities to maximise their learning from the project.

So what do we mean by 'team learning'? Building on the Swieringa and Wierdsma (1992) definition of learning, we describe team learning as the 'changing of team behaviour'. Clearly team learning can only happen as a result of individuals' learning; however this is a necessary, not a sufficient, condition for team learning. There is a need for mutual or collective behavioural changes among the team; it could be, for instance, that as a result of a review of the way project meetings are working, the team decides to run them differently. It could be that as a result of some team members' learning experiences of dealing with their support teams the project team might decide on a new approach to communication or involvement of the support team members.

Senge (1990) puts another perspective on team learning. He draws a distinction between discussion and dialogue. *Discussion* is described as more like a:

> Ping-Pong game where we are hitting the ball back and forward between us. In such a game the subject of common interest may be analysed and dissected from many points of view provided by those that take part...the purpose of the game is normally 'to win' and in this case winning means to have one's views accepted by the group.

Senge then goes on to describe *dialogue* as follows:

> In dialogue...a group accesses a larger 'pool of common meaning' which cannot be accessed individually. 'The whole organises the parts', rather than trying to pull the parts into a whole...In dialogue individuals gain insights that simply could not be achieved individually.

Senge argues that teams need both discussion and dialogue. Discussions are needed to take action, and dialogue is needed to explore and gain a grasp of more complex issues. Much of the time the project team will be involved in discussion. However, there will be occasions when issues surrounding either the project itself or the way the team is working will generate the opportunity for dialogue. The people challenge is to maximise the opportunity for team learning from all aspects of the project team's work.

Strategies for maximising individual and team learning

1 Early in the project life, encourage team members to complete a learning styles questionnaire. There are several on the market, eg the Honey and Mumford Learning Style Questionnaire, or the McBer and Co Learning-Style Inventory.

2 Devote part of a team meeting in the early stage of the project to sharing members' learning styles and discussing the latters' implications for learning from the project.

3 Make maximising individual and team learning a project objective.

4 Put *learning on the agenda* – literally. Consider having a regular section on the agenda of project team meetings for members to comment on their learning experiences and draw out any team learning experiences.

5 Encourage individual team members to keep learning logs – see the suggested format in Table 7. Keep a team learning log in a similar format.

Organisational learning

Like Swieringa and Wierdsma (1992), we see organisational learning as changing organisational behaviour. They describe three levels of organisational learning:

- 'Single-loop learning', which entails bringing about changes in rules. In the context of project working, it would be about learning to operate in and manage projects better.
- 'Double-loop learning' not only brings about changes in rules but also looks at why those rules exist. In the context

Table 7
INDIVIDUAL LEARNING LOGS – SUGGESTED FORMAT

Date	Background to activity/experience	What happened/ outcomes	Reflections – what you learned	How you will apply the learning
10 FEB 199*	Public disagreement with client representative.	I had to go back and apologise to him – try to mend fences.	Need to get more alongside client reps and influence them rather than try to bully them.	I will develop my skill of getting into rapport with the client reps so I can see things from their perspective. (Would probably be helpful with other team members too!)
26 MAR 199*	Needed to be able to prepare detailed resource charts	Attended Microsoft Project advanced training course.	Complex area – need to be very clear on resource data being used. However, potentially a very useful tool for the project team.	I will produce resource charts for the key resources of professional staff first and then discuss them with the project team.
14 APR 199*	Meetings with the support team in my department taking too long and wasting time.	Observed last two meetings carefully – too much time spent on minor issues, so some key issues not discussed effectively because insufficient time.	Need for an agenda with clear outcomes and time allocations required for each item.	I will consult with support team at the next meeting and propose that the agenda is prepared in this way.
etc				

The individual log should be completed as required immediately after the event occurs, while the detail is still fresh in your mind, and not retrospectively.

The team log, in a similar format, should be completed at project team meetings and form part of the permanent record of the meeting. It should be included with the summary of the meeting sent out to all team members.

of project working, the learning would focus on what problems or opportunities are best handled by project working.

☐ 'Triple-loop learning' occurs when the 'essential principles
on which the organisation is founded come into discussion'. This is about questioning such fundamental issues as
what business the organisation should be in, etc.
Sometimes projects are actually aimed at this type of learning, but sometimes it can come about as a by-product. In a
project to improve the quality of service offered by a training department, the outcome might be a fundamental
change of approach – for example, a decision to stop offer-
ing traditional training programmes and move to
self-managed learning.

Single- and sometimes double-loop learning are the intended
outcomes of the type of reviews that take place at the end of
some projects. Frame (1995) calls them 'end-of-project evaluations', which he describes as follows:

> The fundamental role of evaluation at the end of a project is to
> offer us an exercise in lessons learned. By applying these
> lessons to other projects, we can beneficially learn from both
> our mistakes and our successes.

This was a familiar concept to many of our practitioners. For
example, Bater of Rank Xerox talked about 'post-implementa-
tion project reviews'; Robinson of Eastern Group referred to
'project appraisals'; and Vessey of LT to 'project completion
reports'. The ICL *Project Delivery Framework* (Whitfield,
1995) suggests that the overall review of a project be carried
out by the project leader's line management. Geddes *et al*
(1990) call these reviews 'project audits'. However, the impression was that although considered a good idea, they did not
happen very often in practice. Frame (1995) suggests also that
even when such evaluations do take place they are only
'marginally effective because they are perceived as threatening
to those who are being evaluated'. However, it is our experience that people positively want to review their experiences, as
long as it is done with the right objectives and in a constructive way, ie for the learning process and not as a witch-hunt to
apportion blame. There can be enormous frustration at seeing

the same mistakes being made or opportunities missed over and over again on successive projects. The importance of this type of review for organisational learning cannot be overstated. The people challenge is how to carry out a review that maximises organisational learning.

Strategies for maximising organisational learning

1 Make it clear to the project team at the outset that such a review will take place. It should be included in the project plan as a distinct activity with a time-scale. Set the objectives of the review in the context of organisational learning.

2 Inform the manager or steering group responsible for the project that they will be receiving a review report at its end. It is important to sell the benefits of such a review in order both to secure the resources for it and to ensure that the results are used to optimum effect.

3 If possible, include all of the core team in the review process. If team members leave before the review, seek their return for the review session or at least have an exit interview with them to capture their thoughts.

4 Consider involving others, for example the sponsor/client, who brings a clearly valuable user-perspective. However, this should depend on the nature of the relationship – let the team decide. Also, consider involving key members of the support team and other stakeholders.

5 Plan the review session carefully. Consider:

☐ the length of the session. This will depend on the size and complexity of the project.

☐ the structure of the session

☐ who will lead or facilitate the session. It may be useful to use a facilitator external to the team. This will allow everyone to participate fully, including the project leader. It may also help to ensure that the review is conducted objectively so that it does not get hijacked down particular paths or overlook certain issues.

In the session itself, it is essential to focus the team on the objectives of organisational learning. Although the team ought by this time to be skilled in the art of discussion and dialogue, the review will probably raise sensitive and controversial issues. Keeping the emphasis on 'what have we learned, what would we do differently' will help the team deal with these issues in a constructive way. Also, the tendency is to dwell on what went wrong, so encourage the team to begin by focusing on what went well, and why.

Celebrating the end of the project

There is usually no standard process of celebrating the end of a project, but often the project team or project leader will initiate some form of event. Roberts of Eastern Group organised a dinner to say thank-you; Robinson recalled informal celebrations, such as the whole team having a go-karting outing; and May of ICL commented that there were sometimes end-of-project parties. However, May supported our view that the closing down of a project should perhaps be given more attention.

For many team members this phase can represent the end of an important chapter in their working life. Perhaps our title for this section should read 'Celebrating the end of the project *and* moving onwards', because it also represents the starting of a new chapter as well. It is interesting that Roberts of Eastern Group used the term 'wake' – a celebration that captures the curious combination of 'lamentations and merry-making' (*Oxford Paperback Dictionary*, 1979).

Celebrations are traditionally used to mark an achievement or ending of a particular period in life – for example graduation balls, 18th or 21st birthday parties, or retirement celebrations. In fact they also mark transitions in people lives. Graduation balls mark the transition between the education and working phase; 18th or 21st birthday parties symbolise the move from youth to adulthood; and retirement parties celebrate not just the achievement of people's working lives but a move into the new phase of retirement. Brockner (1992) comments:

Sociologists have noted that important changes in people's lives are accompanied by a formal ceremony recognising the transition. It is somehow easier to accept transitions when people take the time to recognise that their world has changed and acknowledge their feelings associated with that change, such as grief, anxiety, and guilt.

The symbolic marking of the transition can be very important in meeting the people challenge of helping them move on from a project. So, the advice is: hold a ceremony!

Strategies for celebrating the end of the project

1 Encourage the team to plan the event – do they want a formal dinner, a party, an outing (one project team went for a day trip to France)? It is important for the team to own the event: there is nothing worse than a party or dinner which people go to for duty's sake.

2 Try to tailor the event in some way to the project and make it fun. For example, some teams do comic reviews or sketches lampooning (gently!) the sponsor, the project leader, members of the team, or memorable events on the project. One team gave awards for memorable team behaviours, eg to the team member who said 'Now hang on a minute' most, or to another team member who was renowned for always being late for project team meetings.

3 Consider recognising people's involvement in the project in some way. This can range from a serious memento – for example, in one project team everyone received a glass engraved with the name of the project – to a more light-hearted one, for example teeshirts printed with a suitable logo.

4 Encourage the team to meet up again after the project ie to have reunions. This is a very valuable way of helping to keep those hard-earned relationships and support networks intact. We are aware of one project team that is still meeting 15 years after the end of the project – is this a record?

Conclusion

The stage of the project team's life cycle of *moving onwards* should be just as challenging and developmental as the earlier stages. It should be a time for celebrating the learning from the project and the challenge of taking that learning into new areas. It should also be the stage of celebrating the relationships that have built up and of taking them forwards as support networks into new jobs and, possibly, new organisations.

That is what we will do now: move on to our next project or perhaps our next book, taking with us the learning we have gained from writing this one and the support networks we have built up through the contributors to our research and the wider support group of all those we have consulted along the way. We shall leave you, the reader, our most important stakeholder, to tackle the people challenges of your project teams. Good luck!

APPENDIX

MEETINGS PROTOCOL

Agenda

DECISIONS REQUIRED

Prepare the agenda before the meeting or at the meeting?

COMMENTS

Preparing the agenda before the meeting allows relevant papers to be circulated and team members to prepare for the items.

Preparing the agenda at the meeting allows discussion of what the most important priorities for inclusion are.

If the agenda is to be prepared before the meeting:
- ☐ Who is to prepare it?
- ☐ By when must agenda items be proposed?
- ☐ By when must the agenda be circulated?
- ☐ How should the order of items be decided?

We would suggest that, in the absence of any other way of sequencing the items, they might be grouped into like areas and these set out in order of importance.

Should all agenda items have:
- ☐ an outcome, eg 'For decision on on ..., discussion, or information ...'
- ☐ a time allowance depending on the importance of the item?

These ensure that the discussion is focused and the outcome achieved.

Setting time-scales helps to plan the most effective use of the time for the meeting – information items should take the least time, discussion items can take the most time.

Chairing the meeting

DECISIONS REQUIRED

Who will chair the meetings?
- ☐ Should it always be the same person, eg the project leader?
- ☐ Should the chair be rotated at each meeting?
- ☐ Should it be the appropriate person for each agenda item?

COMMENTS

The project leader might be considered the best person to chair the meeting because he or she has probably got the best overview of the whole project and might be skilled in chairing meetings.

Rotating the chair may work well in those teams which favour a more democratic approach. It can also allow for the development of chairing skills in all team members.

Chairing by agenda item ensures responsibility for handling that section of the meeting effectively lies with the person who perhaps knows most about the agenda item.

What is the role of the chairperson? Is it
- ☐ to manage the timing of the meeting
- ☐ to summarise the conclusions reached on each item to ensure agreement and commitment
- ☐ to manage the balance of contributions from team members
- ☐ to manage the behaviours according to the agreed groundrules (see below)?

It is important to be explicit about the role of the chairperson.

Recording the meeting

DECISION REQUIRED

POINTS FOR DISCUSSION

What sort of records of the meeting does the team require:
- □ summary of discussion
- □ outcomes
- □ action arising – what, by whom, and by when
- □ formal or legal minutes?

Some project teams favour the shortest and most succinct records possible – usually just outcomes and actions arising.

In other project teams it may be considered important to have a record of the discussion, eg perhaps to prove that all factors were considered when making a decision.

Some teams record outcomes and actions only, with discussion recorded only exceptionally.

There may be a need for formal minutes – for example, on Health and Safety projects.

Who should receive the meeting record?
- □ All members of the project team?
- □ Anyone else, eg support team members, stakeholders?

Normally it would be all the project team members.

It may be worth considering some or all of the support team members – perhaps the ones affected by the outcomes or involved in the action arising.

An important issue is what information the stakeholders, eg the sponsor or customer for the project, need – perhaps only a summary.

Ground rules for behaviour at meetings

DECISIONS REQUIRED

What behaviours are acceptable or unacceptable? For example:

☐ not blocking, interrupting, or talking over another team member

☐ listening actively to everyone, seeking clarification where appropriate

☐ always giving a reason if you disagree with what is said – just saying 'It won't work' is not acceptable

☐ not using defending or attacking behaviours.

COMMENTS

Setting ground rules at the outset and having them visible at every meeting can be a very useful way of ensuring that meetings are well controlled – the best control is self-control!

Reviewing the meeting

DECISION REQUIRED

Will the team review the effectiveness of the meeting:

☐ at all

☐ occasionally

☐ after every meeting?

POINTS FOR DISCUSSION

Many teams set groundrules but see them fall into disuse. It is essential that they are taken seriously. Regular reviews of how the team performed at a meeting can be a useful way of achieving this. The Rackham categories of behaviour as a monitoring process can be helpful (see Rackham and Morgan (1977)).

BIBLIOGRAPHY

ADAIR J. (1983) *Effective leadership*. Aldershot, Gower

ADAIR J. (1986) *Effective teambuilding*. Aldershot, Gower.

ADAIR J. (1997) *Leadership skills*. London, Institute of Personnel and Development.

ARMSTRONG M. (1996) 'How group efforts can pay dividends'. *People Management*. 25 January. pp 22–27.

BEE R. *and* BEE F. (1996) *Constructive feedback*. London, Institute of Personnel and Development.

BELBIN R. M. (1981) *Management teams: why they succeed or fail*. London, Heinemann.

BELBIN R. M. (1993) *Team roles at work*. Oxford, Butterworth-Heinemann Ltd.

BROCKNER J. (1992) 'Managing the effects of layoffs on survivors'. *California Management Review*. Vol. 34, Part 2. pp 9–28.

COVEY S. R. (1992) *The seven habits of highly effective people*. London, Simon & Schuster.

CROFT C. (1996) 'Pushing against a culture of reliance'. *People Management*. 2 May. pp 36–37.

DAVIS S. M. *and* LAWRENCE P. R. (1977) 'Problems of matrix organisations'. *Harvard Business Review*. Vol. 56, No. 3, May-June. pp 131–42.

DRUKER P. F. (1954) *The practice of management*. San Francisco, Harpers.

DRUKER J. *and* WHITE G. (1996) *Managing people in construction*. London, Institute of Personnel and Development.

FARMER P. *and* BEE F. M. (1995) 'HR projects on the right track'. *People Management*. 10 August. pp 28–30.

FRAME J. D. (1995) *Managing projects in organisations*. San Francisco, Jossey-Bass Inc.

GEDDES M., HASTINGS C. *and* BRINER W. (1990) *Project leader-*

ship. Aldershot, Gower

GUIRDHAM M. (1990) *Interpersonal skills at work.* London, Prentice Hall.

HANDY C. B. (1977) *Understanding organisations.* Middlesex, Penguin Books Ltd.

HARDINGHAM A. *and* ROYAL J. (1994) *Pulling together: teamwork in practice.* London, Institute of Personnel and Development.

HERZBERG F. (1966) *Work and the nature of man.* New York, World Publications.

HONEY P. *and* MUMFORD A. (1992) *Manual of learning styles.* Maidenhead, Peter Honey.

HOWELL K. *and* CAMERON E. (1996) 'The benefits of an outsider's opinion'. *People Management.* 8 August. pp 28–30.

ICL. (1995) *See* International Computers Ltd. (1995)

INTERNATIONAL COMPUTERS LTD. (1995) *Project management: career stream.* London.

KOLB D. *et al* (eds). (1974) 'Four styles of managerial learning', in *Organisational Psychology, Book of Readings.* 2nd ed. New York, Prentice Hall International Inc.

LEVESON R. (1996) 'Can professionals be multi-skilled?' *People Management.* 29 August. pp 36–38.

LOCKE E. A. (1968) 'Towards a theory of task motivation and incentives'. *Organisational Behaviour and Human Performance.* Vol. 3. pp 157–89.

LOCKYER K. (1984) *Critical path analysis and other project network techniques.* 4th ed. London, Pitman.

LONDON UNDERGROUND LTD. (1996) Internally circulated MPD document (unpublished).

MACAULAY S. *and* HARDING N. (1996) 'Drawing up a new careers contract'. *People Management.* 4 April. pp 34–35.

MCMASTER M. D. (1986) *Performance management: creating the conditions for results.* Portland Oregon, Metamorphous Press.

MASLOW A. (1970) *Motivation and personality.* 2nd ed. New York, Harper and Row.

OSBORNE A. F. (1957) *Applied imagination.* Revised ed. New York, Charles Scribner.

Oxford Paperback Dictionary. (1979) Compiler: Hawkins J. M.

Oxford, Oxford University Press.

People Management, (LUL Advertisement). 12 September 1996, p 109–10.

PETERS T. (1987) *Thriving on chaos*. London, Pan Books Ltd.

RACKHAM N. *and* MORGAN T.R.G. (1977) *Behaviour analysis in training*. Maidenhead, McGraw-Hill 7.

ROSENAU M. D. Jr. (1992) *Successful project management*. New York, Van Nostrand Reinhold.

SENGE P. (1990) *The fifth discipline: the art and practice of the learning organisation*. London, Century Business.

SWIERINGA J. *and* WIERDSMA A. (1992) *Becoming a learning organisation*. Wokingham, Addison-Wesley Publishing Co.

THOMAS A. (1995) *Coaching for staff development*. Leicester, British Psychological Society Books.

THOMAS K. (1975) 'Conflict and conflict management'. In Marvin Dunette (ed.), *The Handbook of industrial and organisational psychology*. Vol. 2. Chicago, Rand McNally.

WATERIDGE J. (1995) 'IT projects: a basis for success'. *International Journal of Project Management*. June.

WHITFIELD D. J. (ed.). (1995) *Project management: project delivery framework*. London, International Computers Ltd.

WOODCOCK M. (1979) *Team development manual*. Aldershot, Gower.

WOOLMER C. (1996) Article in the *Independent*. London, 21 November.

YOUNG T. L. (1993) *Planning projects: 20 steps to effective project planning*. London, The Industrial Society.

INDEX

Other titles in the Developing Practice series

Telephone your orders to Plymbridge Distributors:
01752 202301

Empowering Team Learning
Enabling ordinary people to do extraordinary things

Michael Pearn

Ordinary people are at the heart of empowered team learning because it is not experts but the people at the 'coalface' who can bring about far-reaching organisational change.

A leading authority on organisational learning, Michael Pearn sets out a breakthrough method that he and his team have developed and that enables people to overcome self-doubt and presumed lack of competence to achieve a high-impact and lasting effect on business success.

- HGV drivers from Shell UK single-handedly conduct a major consultation exercise which leads to a new partnership with management based on openness and trust.
- A shop-floor team from a subsidiary of Alcan International achieves world-class innovation in safety without any expert help.
- A team of unemployed people from the Republic of Ireland undertakes a project matching the needs of employers with the competencies available among the local unemployed.

Drawing on these and other vivid illustrations, the authors provide a compelling vision of what can be achieved by empowered teams. They proceed to equip the reader with step-by-step guidance on how to design and run an effective programme so that the group moves from taking responsibility to generating ideas and implementing their own solutions.

Empowered team learning, the book makes clear, is not only a powerful approach that stimulates and motivates individual members but can also transform groups into creative and skilful agents for change.

1998   176 pages   Pbk   ISBN 0 85292 734 7   **£18.95**

Flexible Working Practices
Techniques and innovations

John Stredwick and Steve Ellis

Flexible working practices can make the difference between survival and success. Introducing flexible working practices can help organisations respond effectively to customer demand, cope with peaks and troughs in activity, recruit and retain the best people, and save significant sums of money. John Stredwick and Steve Ellis build on the experiences of leading-edge companies – from SmithKline Beecham to Siemens GEC, Birds Eye Walls to Xerox, Cable and Wireless to the Co-operative Bank – to help practitioners develop effective policies on:

- temporal flexibility: annual hours, job-sharing, part-time and portfolio working
- predicting the unpredictable: complementary workers, interim managers and new forms of shiftworking
- functional flexibility: multiskilling, outsourcing, teleworking and call centres
- using individual and team reward – competence-based, performance-based and profit-related pay, and gainsharing and broadbanding – to support flexibility
- 'family-friendly' policies: flexitime, career breaks, childcare and eldercare
- clarifying the 'psychological contract' with empowered employees.

A closing chapter pulls together the different options and sets out the main techniques for 'selling' flexibility to a sceptical workforce.

1998   344 pages   Pbk   ISBN 0 85292 744 4   **£18.95**

Performance Management
The new realities

Angela Baron and Michael Armstrong

All employers need to find ways to improve the performance of their people. Yet many of today's personnel departments are abolishing rigid systems of performance management in favour of strategic frameworks that empower individual managers to communicate with, motivate and develop their staff.

Here, one of Britain's best-known business writers and the IPD's Policy Adviser for Employee Resourcing draw on detailed data from over 550 organisations – including the latest innovations adopted by leading-edge companies ranging from BP Exploration to the Corporation of London, and from AA Insurance to Zeneca – to illuminate how approaches to appraisal have evolved and to identify current best practice in performance management. They explore its history, philosophy and separate elements, the criticisms it has attracted and its impact (if any) on quantifiable business results. They also offer practitioners invaluable guidance on:

- the fundamental processes: from target-setting through measurement to performance and development reviews
- performance management skills: coaching, counselling and problem-solving
- meeting developmental needs and enhancing team performance
- paying for performance and competences
- introducing performance management and evaluating its effectiveness.

Throughout, the authors have tailored their suggestions to the practical problems revealed by their research. There could be no better source of support for organisations facing this most crucial challenge.

1998   480 pages   Pbk   ISBN 0 85292 727 4   **£18.95**